messy
spirituality

michael yaconelli

messy spirituality

God's Annoying Love for Imperfect People

ZONDERVAN™

GRAND RAPIDS, MICHIGAN 49530

ZONDERVAN™

Messy Spirituality
Copyright © 2002 by Michael Yaconelli

Requests for information should be addressed to:
Zondervan, *Grand Rapids, Michigan 49530*

Library of Congress Cataloging-in-Publication Data

Yaconelli, Mike.
    Messy spirituality : God's annoying love for imperfect people /
Michael Yaconelli.
       p. cm.
    Includes bibliographical references.
    ISBN 0-310-23533-2
    1. Spirituality.   I. Title.
    BV4501.3 .Y33 2002
    248.4—dc21

                                           2001007125

This edition printed on acid-free paper.

Published in association with the literary agency of Wolgemuth & Associates, Inc.

Interior design by Beth Shagene

Printed in the United States of America

02 03 04 05 06 07 08 /❖ DC/ 10 9 8 7 6 5 4 3 2 1

For my mom,
Marguerite Yaconelli,
who instilled in me a fondness for grace

contents

messy
The Workshop of the Spiritual Life

I stake the future on the few humble and hearty lovers who seek God passionately in the marvelous, messy world of redeemed and related realities that lie in front of our noses.

WILLIAM MCNAMARA

Dear God,
I'm doing the best I can.
Frank

CHILDREN'S LETTERS TO GOD

I go into churches and everyone seems to feel so good about themselves.

    Everyone calls themselves a Christian nowadays. How dare we call ourselves Christians? It's only for Jesus to decide whether we are Christian or not. I don't think He's made a decision in my case, and I'm afraid that when He does I am going to be sent straight to hell. I don't feel I can call myself a Christian. I can't be satisfied with myself. We all seem to be pretty contented with ourselves in church and that makes me sick. I think all this contentment makes Jesus nervous.

ROBERT COLES, *WITTENBURG DOOR*

My life is a mess.

After forty-five years of trying to follow Jesus, I keep losing him in the crowded busyness of my life. I know Jesus is there, somewhere, but it's difficult to make him out in the haze of everyday life.

For as long as I can remember, I have wanted to be a godly person. Yet when I look at the yesterdays of my life, what I see, mostly, is a broken, irregular path littered with mistakes and failure. I have had temporary successes and isolated moments of closeness to God, but I long for the continuing presence of Jesus. Most of the moments of my life seem hopelessly tangled in a web of obligations and distractions.

I want to be a good person. I don't want to fail. I want to learn from my mistakes, rid myself of distractions, and run into the arms of Jesus. Most of the time, however, I feel like I am running away from Jesus into the arms of my own clutteredness.

I want desperately to know God better. I want to be consistent. Right now the only consistency in my life is my inconsistency. Who I want to be and who I am are not very close together. I am not doing well at the living-a-consistent-life thing.

I don't want to be St. John of the Cross or Billy Graham. I just want to be remembered as a person who loved God, who served others more than he served himself, who was trying to grow in maturity and stability. I want to have more victories than defeats, yet here I am, almost sixty, and I fail on a regular basis.

If I were to die today, I would be nervous about what people would say at my funeral. I would be happy if they said things like "He was a nice guy" or "He was occasionally decent" or "Mike wasn't as bad as a lot of people." Unfortunately, eulogies are delivered by people who know the deceased. I know what the consensus would be. "Mike was a mess."

When I was younger, I believed my inconsistency was due to my youth. I believed that age would teach me all I needed to know and that when I was older I would have learned the lessons of life and discovered the secrets of true spirituality.

I *am* older, a lot older, and the secrets are still secret from me.

I often dream that I am tagging along behind Jesus, longing for him to choose me as one of his disciples. Without warning, he turns around, looks straight into my eyes, and says, "Follow me!" My heart races, and I begin to run toward him when he interrupts with, "Oh, not you; the guy behind you. Sorry."

I have been trying to follow Christ most of my life, and the best I can do is a stumbling, bumbling, clumsy kind of following. I wake up most days with the humiliating awareness that I have no clue where Jesus is. Even though I am a minister, even though I think about Jesus every day, my following is . . . uh . . . meandering.

So I've decided to write a book about the spiritual life.

I know what you're thinking. Based on what I've just said about my walk with God, having me write about spirituality is like having Bozo the Clown explain the meaning of the universe, like playing Handel's *Messiah* on the kazoo. How can someone whose life is obviously *unspiritual* presume to talk about spirituality? How can someone unholy presume to talk about holiness? It makes no sense.

Unless. Un*less!* Unless spirituality, as most of us understand it, is not spirituality at all.

Sadly, *spiritual* is most commonly used by Christians to describe people who pray all day long, read their Bibles constantly, never get angry or rattled, possess special powers, and have the inside track to God. *Spirituality,* for most, has an *oth*erworldly ring to it, calling to mind eccentric "saints" who have forsaken the world, taken vows of poverty, and isolated themselves in cloisters.

Nothing wrong with the spirituality of monks. Monks certainly experience a *kind* of spirituality, a way of seeking and knowing God, *but what about the rest of us?* What about those of us who live in the city, have a wife or husband, three children, two cats, and a washing machine that has stopped working? What about those of us who are single, work sixty to seventy hours a week, have parents who wonder why we're not married, and have friends who make much more money than we do? What about those of us who are divorced, still trying to heal from the scars of rejection, trying to cope with the single-parenting of children who don't understand why this has happened to them?

Is there a spirituality for the rest of us who are not secluded in a monastery, who don't have it all together and probably never will?

Spirituality for the Rest of Us

The answer is yes!

What landed Jesus on the cross was the preposterous idea that common, ordinary, broken, screwed-up people *could be godly!* What drove Jesus' enemies crazy were his criticisms of the "perfect" religious people and his acceptance of the imperfect nonreligious people. The shocking implication of Jesus' ministry is that *anyone* can be spiritual.

Scandalous? Maybe.

Maybe truth *is* scandalous. Maybe the scandal is that all of us are in some condition of not-togetherness, even those of us who are trying to be godly. Maybe we're all a mess, not only sinful messy but inconsistent messy, up-and-down messy, in-and-out messy, now-I-believe-now-I-don't messy, I-get-it-now-I-don't-get-it messy, I-understand-uh-now-I-don't-understand messy.

I admit, messy spirituality sounds . . . well . . . un*spiritual*.

Surely there are guidelines to follow, principles to live by, maps to show us where to go, and secrets we can uncover to find a spirituality that is clean and tidy.

I'm afraid not.

Spirituality is not a formula; it is not a test. It is a relationship. Spirituality is not about competency; it is about intimacy. Spirituality is not about perfection; it is about connection. The way of the spiritual life begins where we are *now* in the mess of our lives. Accepting the reality of our broken, flawed lives is the beginning of spirituality not because the spiritual life will remove our flaws but because we *let go* of seeking perfection and, instead, seek God, the one who is present in the tangledness of our lives. Spirituality is not about being fixed; it is about God's being present in the mess of our unfixedness.

Look at the Bible. Its pages overflow with messy people. The biblical writers did not edit out the flaws of its heroes. Like Noah, for example. Everyone thought he was crazy. He certainly *was* a little strange, but Noah was also courageous, a man of great faith and strong will. Against the backdrop of unrelenting ridicule, Noah built a huge ark in the middle of the desert because God told him it was going to rain. No one believed him, but the rains did come and the flood happened, and after the water receded, Noah triumphantly left the boat, *got drunk, and got naked.*[1]

What? *Drunk and naked?* I don't recall any of my Bible teachers or pastors talking about Noah's ... uh ... moment of indiscretion ... er ... weakness ... um ... failure. The Noah I've always heard about was fiercely faithful, irrepressibly independent, and relentlessly resolute. Noah was the model of great faith. Very few ever refer to Noah's losing battle with wine. Maybe being strong and faithful has its downside. Maybe for flood survivors life is more complicated than we would like to think, and maybe even Noah could have bouts of depression and loneliness.

Why should I be surprised? Turns out *all* of the biblical characters were a complex mix of strengths and weaknesses. David, Abraham, Lot, Saul, Solomon, Rahab, and Sarah were God-loving, courageous, brilliant, fearless, loyal, passionate, committed holy men and women who were also murderers, adulterers, and manic depressives. They were men and women who could be gentle, holy, defenders of the faith one minute, and insecure, mentally unstable, unbelieving, shrewd, lying, grudge-holding tyrants the next.

The New Testament characters weren't much better. Look who Jesus hung out with. Prostitutes, tax collectors, adulterers, mental cases, penniless riffraff, and losers of all kinds. His disciples were hardly models of saintliness. They were committed to Jesus, were ready to follow him anywhere (with one notable exception), but they were also troubled by infighting, always jockeying for position, suspicious of each other, accusatory, impulsive, selfish, lazy, and disloyal. Most of the time, they did not understand what Jesus was talking about, and when he died, they had no clue what to do next.

One very clear example of the messiness of the disciples took place in a tiny Samaritan village. On their way to Jerusalem, Jesus and the disciples stopped in this village for the evening. The Samaritans, however, weren't in a mood to cooperate. Most Jews didn't give Samaritans the time of day, so the Samaritans decided to return the favor by making it clear that Jesus and his disciples weren't welcome in their town. James and John (this would be the *beloved* disciple John) were furious, storming up to Jesus with the very undisciplelike question, "Lord, do you want us to call fire down from heaven to destroy them?"[2] Not exactly an example of mature, unmessy discipleship.

You might say Christianity has a tradition of messy spirituality. Messy prophets, messy kings, messy disciples, messy apostles. From God's people getting in one mess after another in the Old Testament to most of the New Testament's being written to straighten out messes in the church, the Bible presents a glorious story of a very messy faith.

Sounds like you and I are in good company.

Messy Spirituality unveils the myth of flawlessness and calls Christians everywhere to come out of hiding and stop pretending.

Messy Spirituality has the audacity to suggest that messiness is the workshop of authentic spirituality, the greenhouse of faith, the place where the real Jesus meets the real us.

Notorious Sinners

A few years ago, I was introduced to a group of uncouth Christians who call themselves "the Notorious Sinners." These are men from all walks of life who meet once a year to openly share their messy spirituality with each other. The title Notorious Sinners refers to the scandalous category of forgiven sinners whose reputations and ongoing flaws didn't seem to keep Jesus away. In fact, Jesus had a habit of collecting disreputables; he called them disciples. He still does. I like people who openly admit their notoriousness—people who unabashedly confess they are hopelessly flawed and hopelessly forgiven. Graciously, these men invited me to be a part of their group.

The Notorious Sinners meet yearly at spiritual-retreat centers, where from the moment we arrive, we find ourselves in trouble with the centers' leadership. We don't act like most contemplatives who come to spiritual-retreat centers—reserved, quiet, silently seeking the voice of God. We're a different kind of contemplative—earthy, boisterous, noisy, and rowdy, tromping around our souls seeking God, hanging out with a rambunctious Jesus who is looking for a good time in our hearts. A number of us smoke cigars, about half are recovering alcoholics, and a couple of the men could embarrass a sailor with their language. Two of the Notorious Sinners show up on their Harleys, complete with leather pants and leather jackets.

I admit I run with a rough crowd—Christians whose discipleship is blatantly real and carelessly passionate, characterized by a brazen godliness. Unafraid to admit their flaws, unintimidated by Christians who deny their own messiness, these guys sometimes look like pagans and other times look like Jesus. They are spiritual troublemakers, really, which is why they look like Jesus (who was always causing trouble himself). They are full of mischief, laughter, and boisterous behavior, which is why they look like pagans. Truly messy disciples. The Notorious Sinners are definitely a bizarre mix of the good, the bad, and the ugly, living a spirituality which defies simple definitions. Oh, and they are some of the most spiritual men I know.

Messy Spirituality is a description of the Christianity most of us live and that few of us admit. It is an attempt to break through the religious wall of secrecy and legitimize a faith which is unfinished, incomplete, and inexperienced. *Messy Spirituality* is a celebration of a discipleship which is under construction.

Messy Spirituality is the scandalous assertion that following Christ is anything but tidy and neat, balanced and orderly. Far from it. Spirituality is complex, complicated, and perplexing— the disorderly, sloppy, chaotic look of authentic faith in the real world.

Spirituality is anything but a straight line; it is a mixed-up, topsy-turvy, helter-skelter godliness that turns our lives into an upside-down toboggan ride full of unexpected turns, surprise bumps, and bone-shattering crashes. In other words, messy spirituality is the delirious consequence of a life ruined by a Jesus who will love us right into his arms.

The Scandal of Spirituality

Jesus is not repelled by us, no matter how messy we are, regardless of how incomplete we are. When we recognize that Jesus is not discouraged by our humanity, is not turned off by our messiness, and simply doggedly pursues us in the face of it all, what else can we do but give in to his outrageous, indiscriminate love?

Anne Lamott, a fellow messy Christian, describes perfectly what happens when Jesus pursues us. In her book *Traveling Mercies*, Anne recounts her conversion to Jesus. Things were not going well in her life: addicted to cocaine and alcohol, involved in an affair that produced a child whom she aborted, helplessly watching her best friend die of cancer. During this time, Anne visited a small church periodically. She would sit in the back to listen to the singing and then leave before the sermon. During the week of her abortion, she spiraled downward.

Disgusted with herself, she drowned her sorrows in alcohol and drugs. She had been bleeding for many hours from the abortion and finally fell into bed, shaky and sad, smoked a cigarette, and turned off the light.

> After a while, as I lay there, I became aware of someone with me, hunkered down in the corner, and I just assumed it was my father, whose presence I had felt over the years when I was frightened and alone. The feeling was so strong that I actually turned on the light for a moment to make sure no one was there— of course, there wasn't. But after a while, in the dark again, I knew beyond any doubt that it was Jesus. I felt him as surely as I feel my dog lying nearby as I write this.
>
> And I was appalled. . . . I thought about what everyone would think of me if I became a Christian, and it seemed an utterly impossible thing that simply could not be allowed to happen. I turned to the wall and said out loud, "I would rather die."
>
> I felt him just sitting there on his haunches in the corner of my sleeping loft, watching me with patience and love, and I squinched my eyes shut, but that didn't help because that's not what I was seeing him with.
>
> Finally I fell asleep, and in the morning, he was gone.
>
> This experience spooked me badly, but I thought it was just an apparition, born of fear and self-loathing and booze and loss of blood. But then everywhere I went, I had the feeling that a little cat was following me, wanting me to reach down and pick it up, wanting me to open the door and let it in. But I knew what would happen: you let a cat in one time, give it a little milk, and then it stays forever. . . .

And one week later, when I went back to church, I was so hungover that I couldn't stand up for the songs, and this time I stayed for the sermon, which I just thought was so ridiculous, like someone trying to convince me of the existence of extraterrestrials, but the last song was so deep and raw and pure that I could not escape. It was as if the people were singing in between the notes, weeping and joyful at the same time, and I felt like their voices or *something* was rocking me in its bosom, holding me like a scared kid, and I opened up to that feeling—and it washed over me.

I began to cry and left before the benediction, and I raced home and felt the little cat running along at my heels, and I walked down the dock past dozens of potted flowers, under a sky as blue as one of God's own dreams, and I opened the door to my houseboat, and I stood there a minute, and then I hung my head and said, . . . "I quit." I took a long deep breath and said out loud, "All right. You can come in."

So this was my beautiful moment of conversion.[3]

Anne Lamott is the most improbable candidate for spirituality I could imagine, until I consider my own candidacy. Anne Lamott seems hopelessly messed up until I remember the mess of my own life. I recognize "the little cat running along" at her heels. He's the same "cat" who's been hounding this messy follower of Christ all his life. No matter how hard I've tried, I've never been able to shake him. You won't be able to shake him either. So we might as well give up, as Anne did, and let "the cat" in. Then we can decide what we're going to do with the not-so-little Jesus who, running wild in our hearts, will wreak havoc in our souls, transforming our messy humanity into a messy spirituality.

2

messy spirituality

The Place Where Our Messiness and Jesus Meet

When we sin and mess up our lives, we find that God doesn't go off and leave us—he enters into our trouble and saves us.

EUGENE PETERSON, *A LONG OBEDIENCE IN THE SAME DIRECTION*

I myself walked up to the Ragman. I told him my name with shame, for I was a sorry figure next to him. Then I took off all my clothes in that place, and I said to him with a dear yearning in my voice: "Dress me."

He dressed me, my Lord, he put new rags on me, and I am a wonder beside him.

WALTER WANGERIN, *RAGMAN AND OTHER CRIES OF FAITH*

Our churches are filled with people who outwardly look contented and at peace but inwardly are crying out for someone to love them ... just as they are—

confused, frustrated, often frightened, guilty, and often unable to communicate even within their own families. But the other people in the church look so happy and contented that one seldom has the courage to admit his own deep needs before such a self-sufficient group as the average church meeting appears to be.

KEITH MILLER

He who thinks that he is finished is finished. How true. Those who think that they have arrived, have lost their way. Those who think they have reached their goal, have missed it. Those who think they are saints, are demons.

HENRI NOUWEN, *THE GENESEE DIARY*

One of my favorite *Peanuts* cartoons starts with Lucy at her five-cent psychology booth, where Charlie Brown has stopped for advice about life.

"Life is like a deck chair, Charlie," she says. "On the cruise ship of life, some people place their deck chair at the rear of the ship so they can see where they've been. Others place their deck chair at the front of the ship so they can see where they're going."

The good "doctor" looks at her puzzled client and asks, "Which way is your deck chair facing?"

Without hesitating, Charlie replies glumly, "I can't even get my deck chair unfolded."

Charlie and I are soul mates.

Everywhere I look on the cruise ship of Christianity, I see crews of instructors, teachers, experts, and gurus eager to explain God's plan for the placement of my deck chair, but I still can't even unfold it. No wonder, when I peruse the titles in a Christian bookstore, I feel like I am the only klutz in the kingdom of God, a spiritual nincompoop lost in a shipful of brilliant biblical thinkers, an ungodly midget in a world of spiritual giants. When I compare my life with the experts', I feel sloppy, unkempt, and messy in the midst of immaculately dressed saints ... *and I'm a minister.* Maybe that's why God allowed me to pastor a church "for people who don't like to go to church." When your "pastor" was kicked out of two Bible colleges, maybe it's easier for people not to be intimidated by some ideal of spirituality.

Many of those who attend our church have always wanted to go to church, wanted to know God better, longed for a better relationship with Jesus, but more often than not, they would end up at a church where they were made to feel as if the "mess" of their lives disqualified them from the possibility of an authentic spiritual life. Let me describe for you the "messy" lives of those who might be sitting in our church on any given Sunday.

Rene: after thirty years of marriage, her husband left her for a younger woman, right after Rene was diagnosed with lung cancer. Devastated and alone, she is slowly trying to follow Jesus in the wreckage of her situation. She was made to feel guilty by her former church because her marriage fell apart. Her faith didn't heal the cancer, her children are not in a good place, and she is having bouts of depression (which "spiritual" Christians shouldn't have, according to her "spiritual" friends), wondering what happened to the good life God was supposed to provide her with.

Darrell: struggling with a long history of abuse and drugs, he usually finds his way to church after a night of drinking. Darrell sits in the last row in a seat close to the door because he doesn't want people to see his swollen face, his red eyes, his unshaven beard. He's ashamed that he cannot tame his drinking problem. He has been told at other churches that if he were totally committed to living a spiritual life, drinking wouldn't be a problem. Trying doesn't count, his church friends have said to him.

Carol: divorced, alone. She went through hell last year dealing with a dying father who required too much of her time because other family members refused to do their part. Now in the aftermath she is left with guilt and anger and the struggle to understand what spirituality looks like in the midst of her ragged and weary day-to-day life. She was told by many of her friends in her previous church that spiritual people don't get divorces, get angry, feel guilty, or resent their families.

Gary and Linda, Carl and Doreen: two of many couples who are facing midlife crises, empty nest syndromes, and the haunting question, "Is this all there is?" These couples are besieged with doubts about Christianity. In their previous church experiences, they were reminded repeatedly that spiritual people don't have midlife crises, nor are they haunted by doubts and fears, because Jesus is the answer to all their questions and insecurities.

Lillian, Regina, Don, and Barbara: older members of our church whose spouses have died. They have decided they are too old to start a new relationship, they feel patronized but not befriended, and they wonder if their last years will be lived out alone.

The list could go on and on. Sprinkled throughout our congregation are good people who have been paralyzed by feelings of inadequacy and unworthiness, insecurity and self-doubt, insignificance and guilt, which are what cripples most of us who are trying to follow Christ.

What Does Messy Spirituality Look Like?

This may sound shocking to some, but spirituality is a home for those who don't have life figured out, who don't know the

Bible as well as they could, and who don't have their spiritual lives all together—*the rest of us* who thought there wasn't a "rest of us," Christians who are *trying to follow Jesus the best we can.*

A couple of years ago, my wife and I sat across the table from a woman we highly respect, a deeply spiritual lady who had profoundly impacted our lives. This woman spent most of her life resisting the noise and activity of the world to seek God in silence and solitude. She had spent hundreds of weeks in silent retreat. This was a woman so saturated with her faith, you could almost smell God when she came into the room.

We were talking about prayer. "It's embarrassing to be sitting with you," I blurted. "You spend days, weeks, even months in prayer. I'm lucky if I spend ten minutes. Compared to you, I'm not very spiritual, I'm afraid."

Her eyes, flashing with anger, caught mine, and she fired back, "Oh, Mike, knock it off. First of all, you don't spend every day with me. You don't know me at all. You are comparing what you know about yourself to what you don't know about me. Secondly, I battle depression daily, and it has won during several periods of my life. I never told you about it. I don't have a family; I like to be alone and silent. Trust me, I am just as 'unspiritual' as you are."

Then she said gently, "You think about God all the time, right?"

"Well, sort of," I said.

"Thinking about God is being with God. Being with God is spirituality. Thinking about God is praying. So shut up with this guilt stuff; you have been praying most of your life! You are a spiritual person!"

What? I've been praying most of my life? What was she talking about? It never occurred to me that Paul's "pray without ceasing" might actually be possible. It never occurred to me that praying could include thinking, that praying could be done with my eyes *open,* that praying could be done standing, sitting, driving, dancing, skiing, lying down, jogging, working. How could anyone accuse *me* of praying all the time when I didn't pray all the time . . . unless my friend was right, unless I was praying without ceasing?

How could anyone accuse me of being spiritual unless spirituality comes in unlimited shapes and sizes, unless spirituality looks like whatever you and I look like when we're thinking about Jesus, when we are trying to find Jesus, when we are trying to figure out what real Christianity looks like in the real world?

Spirituality looks like whatever you and I look like when we're thinking about Jesus, when we are trying to find Jesus, when we are trying to figure out what real Christianity looks like in the real world.

Unpretending

There is no room for pretending in the spiritual life. Unfortunately, in many religious circles, there exists an unwritten rule. Pretend. Act like God is in control when you don't believe he is. Give the impression everything is okay in your life when it's not. Pretend you believe when you doubt; hide your imperfections; maintain the image of a perfect marriage with healthy and well-adjusted children when your family is like any other normal dysfunctional family. And whatever you do, don't admit that you sin.

Practically, pretending is efficient, uncomplicated, and quick. Answering "Fine" to the question "How are you doing?" is much easier and quicker than saying, "Not very well, thank you; my back is bothering me, my teenage children are disappointing me, I'm unhappy with my body, my husband never speaks to me, and I'm wondering if Christianity is true."

Honesty requires a huge investment of time and energy from the person asking the question (who would then wish they'd never asked).

Pretending is the grease of modern nonrelationships. Pretending perpetuates the illusion of relationships by connecting us on the basis of who we aren't. People who pretend have pretend relationships. But being real is a synonym for messy spirituality, because when we are real, our messiness is there for everyone to see.

Some people consider the use of words like *messy spirituality* rude and audacious. "How dare you suggest that people are messy? What are you proposing? Are you suggesting that sin is okay, that we should condone less than a 100 percent effort to serve God? You are too negative. It's not helpful to emphasize our flaws."

But the truth is, we *are* a mess. None of us is who we appear to be. We all have secrets. We all have issues. We all struggle from time to time. No one is perfect. Not one. (I have just paraphrased Romans 3:10.) The essence of messy spirituality is the refusal to pretend, to lie, or to allow others to believe we are something we are not. Unfortunately, people can handle the most difficult issues more easily than they can handle the lack of pretending.

When you and I stop pretending, we expose the pretending of everyone else. The bubble of the perfect Christian life is burst, and we all must face the reality of our brokenness.

When my eighteen-month-old daughter was diagnosed with cancer, I was unprepared for the pretending of my Christian friends. Within hours of the news getting out, I was inundated with statements like, "I'm sure God is doing this for a reason. God can heal your daughter if you just have faith. Even if she dies, she will be better off." I remember answering these people, "I hope God is *not* doing this. I don't believe

God promises to heal my daughter. Certainly dying is never better than living, otherwise we should all commit suicide." You can imagine the responses of those around me. They wrote off my statements to shock, bitterness, cynicism, and lack of faith. But I *wasn't* bitter; I *wasn't* cynical. I was *telling the truth*. I could not, *would not* pretend anymore.

Was I confused about exactly where God was? Of course. Did I have serious questions about my faith? Yes. Was I desperate, depressed, angry, resentful? Yes, I was all those things. I only wish others could have given me the space to be honest and that they could have been honest too. I look back now, twenty-nine years later, and I realize these people were confused and afraid themselves. If they could get me to agree with them, then they would no longer be afraid. But I couldn't do it. They were forced to deal with the reality of an eighteen-month-old baby who could have died from a terrible disease. (She is very much alive, by the way.) Even today, if you were to ask me why my daughter lived, I would have only one answer: "I don't know." I watched a lot of children Lisa's age die during the same period that she was ill, and for the life of me, I don't know where God was. I cannot pretend the mystery of God away.

Sermons are not always amazing masterpieces of truth, wit, and insight. Sometimes the sermon just doesn't work, doesn't connect. It just lies there in a pile while the minister desperately tries to resuscitate it. I was having one of those Sundays. My sermon was just not connecting, people were bored, looking at their watches, and at one point, almost in unison, a majority of the congregation looked back at the clock on the wall. I had no choice; I had to admit the truth.

"I . . . uh . . . realize I've gone a little long today. Sorry, but I have just one more point I'd like to make."

Sadie, lovely honest Sadie, threw her hands to her face and yelled, "Oooh nooo!" causing the rest of the congregation to laugh . . . and then applaud. Most people were trying to stifle what they were really feeling, but not Sadie. Luckily her condition of Down's syndrome doesn't allow her to understand pretending, so she said not only what she thought but what everyone else thought as well.

The sermon was over. Thank God . . . and thank Sadie.

Spiritual people tell the truth.

Unfinishedness

Spiritual people also admit their unfinishedness. Unfinished means incomplete, imperfect, in process, in progress, under construction. Spiritual describes someone who is incomplete, imperfectly living their life for God. The construction site of our souls exposes our flaws, the rough-hewn, not-finished faith clearly visible in our hearts. When we seek God, Jesus begins to take shape in our lives. He *begins* a good work in us, he *starts* changing us, but the finishing process is a more-than-a-lifetime process. The work of God in our lives *will never be finished* until we meet Jesus face to face. The author of Hebrews wrote, "Let us fix our eyes on Jesus, the author and perfecter [or finisher] of our faith."[1] Spirituality isn't about being finished and perfect; spirituality is about trusting God in our unfinishedness.

I'll never forget the day Eric, a recovering alcoholic, stood up in our church during announcements. Eric's lifelong battle with alcohol had been mostly unsuccessful. He had been in and out of jail, and his drinking was taking its toll on his marriage.

"I need prayer," he said. "My wife has given me an ultimatum—drinking or her. She's asked me to decide today, and I just wanted to tell you all that I have decided . . ."

A long awkward pause ensued, and every person in the church was on the edge of their seat with their face turned toward him, encouraging him, pleading with him to make the right decision. You could have heard a pin drop.

Finally, he stumbled on, tears in his eyes. "I've decided to choose my wife!"

Applause and cheering broke out. No one said it, but you could hear it anyway: "Good answer! Good answer!" Eric was not afraid to tell the truth; he was not afraid to reveal to all of us how difficult it was to give up alcohol, even for his wife. Eric is a spiritual man. Troubled? Yes. Weak? Yes. Unfinished? Absolutely! But Eric told the truth and admitted that his desire for drinking was conflicting with his desire to stay married. Eric refused to pretend life is clean and neat, and he knew he had to tell us the way things were, not the way we wished they were.

Jesus understood unfinishedness very well, which is why he was comfortable leaving eleven unfinished disciples. When he died, the disciples were confused, depressed, afraid, and doubtful. They faced a lifetime of finishing, just like you and me. Messy spirituality not only reminds us we will always be a work in progress; it also reminds us that the unfinished life is a lot more spiritual than we imagined.

Incompetence

Messy spirituality describes our godly incompetence. No one does holy living very well. Spirituality is the humiliating recognition that I don't know how to pray well. I don't understand God's Word or know how to navigate it properly, and I don't know how to competently live out my commitment to Christ. Messy spirituality affirms our spiritual clumsiness.

I grew up in a church where dancing was frowned upon. As a result, four decades later, I still can't dance. Even worship dancing causes my heart to race because I am desperately afraid of anyone seeing my stiff, awkward attempts to make my body move. Because I am a lousy dancer, I avoid any experience in which dancing is a possibility.

When it comes to the spiritual life, I am amazed how many of us don't know how to dance. We stand before God, the music starts playing, and we are embarrassed by our incompetence. The church has communicated that competence is one of the fruits of the Spirit and that, therefore, spiritual people are supposed to live faith competently. So many people are afraid of embracing the spiritual life because of the possibility they might say or do the incompetent thing.

One Sunday morning, Gary, a new Christian in our church, offered to read the Scripture for the day, which was the second chapter of Acts. During the worship service, I could see him in the front row, Bible in hand, checking the bulletin to make sure he wouldn't miss his moment. When the time came, Gary stood in front of the congregation and thumbed through his Bible, searching for the book of Acts . . . and searching . . . and searching. Finally, after two awkward minutes, he turned around and said sheepishly, "Uh, I can find the first book of Acts, but where is the second book of Acts?" Everyone laughed and someone graciously led him to the second *chapter* of the only book of Acts in the Bible. Luckily, our church is a church which expects incompetence.

Jesus responds to desire. Which is why he responded to people who interrupted him, yelled at him, touched him, screamed obscenities at him, barged in on him, crashed through ceilings to get to him. *Jesus cares more about desire than about competence.*

My hunch is most of you reading this book feel incompetent *and* you can't let go of Jesus. Jesus sees right through your incompetence into a heart longing for him.

It was time for the Scripture reading and a girl shuffled toward the front of the church. What a moment for Connie. She had finally mustered enough courage to ask the pastor if she could read the Scripture. Without hesitation, he said yes. For years Connie had stifled her desire to serve in the church because of her "incompetencies." Reading was extremely difficult for her, and Connie had a terrible time enunciating clearly. But she had been in this church many years, and she was beginning to understand the grace of God. Jesus didn't die just for our sins; he died so people who couldn't read or speak could read and speak. Now she could serve the Jesus she loved so much. Now she could express her desire for God in a tangible way.

Connie's steps were labored as she made her way to the front; one leg was shorter than the other, causing her body to teeter from side to side. Finally, she was standing up front, looking at the congregation with pride and joy.

The congregation was silent. Too silent.

The screaming silence was covering up the congregation's discomfort. Clearly, most of them were trying to understand what Connie was doing, and they were trying not to notice her many incompetencies. Her eyes were too close together, and her head twisted back and forth at odd angles while her face wrenched from one grimace to another.

Connie began to read, and stammering, stuttering, she stumbled proudly through the passage in a long sequence of untranslatable sounds, garbled sentences, long tortuous pauses, and jumbled phrases. Finally, the reading was over, and the congregation was exhausted.

Connie didn't notice the exhaustion. She was ecstatic. Her face seemed no longer distorted, only full of joy. Her cheeks were flush with pride; her eyes were sparkling with the joy of accomplishment; her heart was warm with knowing she had *served* the congregation, participated in her faith. Yes, she would remember this day for a long time. How wonderful it was, she thought, to no longer be a *spectator* in church; she *was* the church this morning!

Thank God her mental capacities were limited. Thank God she was not able to discern the faces of the congregation or she would have crumbled in despair. Thank God she wasn't able to sense what people were really thinking.

Almost everyone in the congregation was thinking, *This is an outrage!* I know this is what they were thinking, because the senior pastor, my father, was ordered to attend an emergency board meeting after the service.

"How did this happen?" they demanded to know. "What were you thinking?"

"Connie wanted to read the Scripture," he replied softly.

"Well, let her stand at the door and pass out bulletins, or help in the mailroom, but don't have her read! The girl can't read or speak. Her reading took ten minutes! The church," they said, "is not a place for incompetence."

My father believes, as I do, that the church *is* the place where the incompetent, the unfinished, and even the unhealthy are welcome. I believe Jesus agrees.

Desperateness

Christianity is not for people who think religion is a pleasant distraction, a nice alternative, or a positive influence. Messy spirituality is a good term for the place where desperation meets Jesus. More often than not, in Jesus' day, desperate people who tried to get to Jesus were surrounded by religious people who either ignored or rejected those who were seeking to have their hunger for God filled. Sadly, not much has changed over the years.

Desperate people don't do well in churches. They don't fit, and they don't cooperate in the furthering of their starvation. "Church people" often label "desperate people" as strange and unbalanced. But when desperate people get a taste of God, they can't stay away from him, no matter what everyone around them thinks.

Desperate is a strong word. That's why I like it. People who are desperate are rude, frantic, and reckless. Desperate people are explosive, focused, and uncompromising in their desire to get what they want. Someone who is desperate will crash through the veil of niceness. The New Testament is filled with desperate people, people who barged into private dinners, screamed at Jesus until they had his attention, or destroyed the roof of someone's house to get to him. People who are desperate for spirituality very seldom worry about the mess they make on their way to be with Jesus.

Barbara Brown Taylor pastored a downtown church for many years. The sanctuary was open during the day, but unfortunately, because of the kind of world we live in, a closed-circuit camera was installed to monitor what went on inside. The receptionist of the church checked the monitor throughout the day.

One day during a staff meeting, the receptionist interrupted to report, "There's a man lying face down on the altar steps. I wouldn't bother you, but he's been there for hours. Every now and then he stands up, raises his arms toward the altar, and lies down again." One of the staff went out to speak to the man, to find out if he was okay, and reported, "He says he's praying." They decided to leave the man alone. But he returned every day, lying on the altar steps. His clothes were worn and dirty; his hair was in knots. The staff instructed the sexton and the altar guild not to disturb the man and to work around him.

Finally, it was Sunday, and as Barbara entered the sanctuary for the early service, she saw the man blocking her path to the altar. She was afraid. What if he was crazy? She approached him cautiously, noticing how dirty he was, how emaciated he was from lack of food. She explained to him that a service was to begin in a few minutes and he would have to leave. He lifted his forehead from the floor and, speaking with a heavy Haitian accent, said, "That's okay."

Barbara describes what happened after he left:

> The eight o'clock service began on time. The faithful took their places and I took mine. We read our parts well. We spoke when we were supposed to speak and were silent when we were supposed to be silent. We offered up our symbolic gifts, we performed our bounden duty and service, and there was nothing wrong with what we did, nothing at all. We were good servants, careful and contrite sinners who had come for our ritual cleansing, but one of us was missing. He had risen and gone his way, but the place where he lay on his face for hours—making a spectacle of himself—seemed all at once so full of heat and light that I stepped around it on my way out, chastened if only for that moment by the call to a love so excessive, so disturbing, so beyond the call to obedience that it made me want to leave all my good works behind.[2]

I wish the man had been invited to stay for the worship service. Maybe Barbara did invite him and he declined. Regardless, I believe Jesus would have asked him to stay. In any case, a desperate man, covered with dirt and hair clotted from days of abuse, filled a sanctuary with the spectacle of God's presence.

When the Unqualified Are Qualified

Walking by a pet shop on his way to school, a young boy stopped and stared through the window. Inside were four black puppies playing together. After school he ran home and pleaded with his mother to let him have one of the puppies. "I'll take care of it, Mom, I will. If you can just give me an advance on my allowance, I'll have enough money to buy one with my own money. Please, Mom, please."

The mother, knowing full well the complications having a new puppy would bring to a busy household, could not resist her son. "Okay, you can get the puppy, but I will expect you to take care of it."

"Yes, Mom, I will." Filled with excitement, the little boy ran to the pet shop to buy his new puppy.

After determining that the boy had enough money, the pet shop owner brought him to the window to choose his puppy. After a few minutes, the young boy said, "Um . . . I'll take the little one in the corner."

"Oh no," said the shop owner, "not that one; he's crippled. Notice how he just sits there; something is wrong with one of his legs, so he can't run and play like the rest of the puppies. Choose another one."

Without saying a word, the boy reached down, lifted his pant leg to expose a chrome leg brace to the owner.

"No," he said firmly, "I think I'll take the puppy in the corner."[3]

It turned out that what disqualified the puppy from being chosen by others is what most qualified him to be chosen by the little boy.

It's amazing how few of us believe in the unqualified grace of God. Oh, yes, God loves us, as long as we're clean and whole and fixed. But it turns out that what disqualifies you and me from "spirituality"—the mess of our lives and our crippledness—is what most qualifies us to be chosen by Jesus.

The Myth of Fixing Ourselves

For a period of time, we were lucky enough to have a house-keeper. She would come in once a week to dust, vacuum, and clean every little out-of-the-way corner of our house. I dreaded the day she came, because my wife and I would spend all morning *cleaning the house for the housekeeper!* We didn't want the house to be dirty, or what would the housekeeper think?!

We act the same way with God. We talk our way out of the spiritual life by refusing to come to God as we are. Instead, we decide to wait until we are ready to come to God as we aren't. We decide that the way we lived yesterday, last week, or last year makes us "damaged goods" and that until we start living "right," we're not "God material." Some of us actually believe that until we choose the correct way to live, we aren't chooseable, that until we clean up the mess, Jesus won't have anything to do with us. The opposite is true. *Until we admit we are a mess,* Jesus won't have anything to do with us. Once we admit how unlovely we are, how unattractive we are, how lost we are, Jesus shows up unexpectedly. According to the New Testament, Jesus is attracted to the unattractive. He prefers the lost ones over the found ones, the losers over the winners, the broken instead of the whole, the messy instead of the unmessy, the crippled instead of the noncrippled.

Dancing the Undanceable

Lost in my thoughts, I was sitting in a hotel ballroom with fifteen hundred college students participating in a weekend faith conference. On the last day of the conference, with school starting the following Monday, the students made it clear they wanted to prolong the conference as long as possible. They wanted to party, to dance the afternoon away, to celebrate the Lord of the dance—to resist going back into the busyness and demands of college life. The morning general session turned into a spontaneous celebration. Young men and women raised their hands, stood on chairs, shouted, cried, and laughed, and then suddenly a conga line broke out. Within seconds, hundreds of college students were weaving in and out of the room in long, raucous lines praising their God.

An older man with cerebral palsy sat in a motorized wheelchair, watching everyone else party. (He wasn't a college student. Technically he wasn't even supposed to be at the conference.) I was seated next to him, watching the students celebrate, when suddenly the wheelchair lunged into the celebration. The man's arms waved, his chair careened around the room with a jerky, captivating motion, his mouth struggled open and shut making incomprehensible sounds. Somehow a man who couldn't dance had become part of the graceful dancing of the crowd. Without warning, his motorized wheelchair lurched to the base of the stage, racing back and forth through a series of figure eights, twirls, and circles. He was laughing, lost in the joy of the Lord. His joy had taken a cold, ugly piece of motorized machinery and transformed it into an extension of his unconfined worship. He and his wheelchair had become one, a dancing, living thing. This man with a crippled body found a way to dance the undanceable.

I envy him. I want my crippled soul to escape the cold and sterile spirituality of a religion where only the perfect nondisabled get in. I want to lurch forward to Jesus, where the unwelcome receive welcome and the unqualified get qualified. I want to hear Jesus tell me I can dance when everyone else says I can't. I want to hear Jesus walk over and whisper to this handicapped, messy Christian, "Do you want to dance?"

3

resisting
the resisters
Overcoming the Saboteurs of Spirituality

Our deepest fear is not that we are inadequate. Our deepest fear is that we are powerful beyond measure. It is our light, not our darkness, that most frightens us. We ask ourselves, Who am I to be brilliant, gorgeous, talented, and fabulous? Actually, who are you not to be? You are a child of God. Your playing small doesn't serve the world. There is nothing enlightened about shrinking so that other people won't feel insecure around you.

NELSON MANDELA

They were good in the worst sense of the word.

MARK TWAIN

No punishment anyone might inflict on them could possibly be worse than the punishment they inflict on themselves by conspiring in their own diminishment.

PARKER PALMER, *LET YOUR LIFE SPEAK*

A blind man sits by the roadside begging. Suddenly, a huge crowd moves down the road, jostling past him. He asks some questions and realizes Jesus is passing by.

His heart begins to race. *Jesus of Nazareth! This is the one they say can heal blindness! All my life I have wanted to see, and my chance is now.* He gets to his feet and yells, "Jesus, Son of David, have mercy on me!"[1]

Instantly the crowd shouts at the blind man, "Shut up! Keep quiet!" Everyone around the man tries to silence him, to keep him from creating a scene, to keep him from "annoying" Jesus.

It is the nature of human beings, the nature of modern life, to silence those who interrupt our routine activities and understandings. We don't like those who speak up, who leave the status quo, who refuse to keep quiet, who reject compliance as a way of life. We would much rather have people shut up than say disturbing things about genuine faith.

The Silencers

Religious institutions do not like surprises and especially dislike a spirituality which threatens the status quo. Threaten others with a loud and boisterous faith, and you will be politely (at first) asked to quiet down; dance your faith instead of sitting still in your pew, and you will be asked to leave; talk about your faith with passion, and you will get expressions of concern about the inappropriateness of your emotions. Allow others to see your brokenness, and you will be reprimanded for being too open; hear the music of faith, and you will be warned of the danger of emotional instability.

Shel Silverstein has written a wonderful poem about those who have been silenced, called "The One Who Stayed." In his brilliantly creative twist on the Pied Piper, we are told about a man who "piped away the kiddies." All the children of Hamlin Town leave—"dancin', spinnin', turnin'"—except for one boy who stayed home. His father affirmed his son's refusal to follow the Pied Piper. The father said his son was lucky he wasn't found by the Piper's music or he would have been "witch-cast like all the rest." But the son knew better. He knew the Piper's music had stirred something in him, something life-giving, and that he would regret silencing his longings to follow him:

> I cannot say I did not hear
> That sound so haunting hollow—
> I heard, I heard, I heard it clear . . .
> I was afraid to follow.[2]

Pity the one who stayed. Cry a tear for the one who heard and was afraid to follow. Mourn the one who let the town grow old around him. Pity all of us who are surrounded by those who are afraid to follow the "sad stranger," the one who came to get us all "dancin', spinnin', turnin'."

But those of us who have heard the haunting sound of Jesus' voice, those who sense life and hope and adventure in the gospel, those who are willing to speak up, to question the deadness around us, to express our desire for life, we must not keep quiet, even if everyone around us tells us we are crazy.

And the crowd *will* call you crazy.

And the masses will try to silence you.

I was speaking at a conference recently and mentioned that a woman in my church—whom I deeply respect and who is one of the most godly women I know—smokes and some-times uses colorful language. After the talk, I was made aware of a pastor in the audience who was outraged by my messages. He was so angry he demanded that everyone from his church no longer listen to my talks.

After the conference, trying to understand what he was so upset about, I contacted him.

"How dare you tell the audience that one of the 'most godly' women you know smokes and uses the language of the world!" he said quite heatedly.

"Because she *is* one of the most godly women I know, and she does happen to smoke and use colorful language," I replied.

The conversation went on for a long time, and he was not impressed with my defense. Although he didn't put it this way, what he was saying was clear: "Godly women do not smoke, nor do they use 'colorful' language! Period." In his spiritual world, there is no place for smoking, swearing, godly women. He didn't want to hear otherwise. No exceptions.

In the real world where I live, this woman is not an exception and remains one of the most godly women I know.

The Assault of the Comfortable

All of us tend to seek comfort, to structure predictability, to eliminate the new and different from our experience. The word *messy* strikes fear into the hearts of the comfortable. According to the comfortable, God does what he always does. "God is the same yesterday, today, and tomorrow," which they interpret as "stays the same." There are those in the church who honestly believe God is a nice and neat God. One quick run through the Bible gives you a different picture. The God of the Bible is the master of surprises: frightening clouds of smoke and fire, earthquakes, windstorms and firestorms, donkeys that talk, pillars of salt, oceans splitting apart, using a little boy to kill a giant, the Messiah in swaddling clothes and dying on a cross. No one can follow God and be comfortable for long.

An attractive young woman on the fast track toward a lucrative business career decided she wanted to delay her career plans in order to work with inner-city young people. God had been working in her heart, and she felt a real sense of calling. She was hired by a church where the ethnic mix was changing, and within weeks she was working with gang members. She successfully convinced a few of them to attend a Bible study at the church. One night she was talking about Matthew 6:33 ("But seek first his kingdom and his righteousness"), explaining that if you want to be a disciple of Jesus, nothing can be more important than him. Her words were, "If the gang is more important than Jesus, then the gang has to go. If your girlfriend is more important than Jesus, then the girlfriend has to go." One of the gang members was so into what she was saying that, after hearing those words, he reacted violently by throwing his arms back, yelling, "Dude, it's hard to be a disciple!" and his elbow crashed through a window. When the church found out, they were very upset at having to pay twenty-six dollars to fix the window, and they restricted the gang members from using the room. Here was a young woman teaching gang members about Jesus, and they were listening. She was doing such a good job that her students understood how costly faith is. What a teacher! But all the *church* could think about were broken windows.

But it gets worse.

A few weeks later, the pastor accidentally interrupted one of the Bible studies. He sat down and spent a few minutes talking with the gang members. After he left, one of the guys said, "Hey, I like that guy. Let's go to church this Sunday." The youth worker decided to seat them in the balcony rather than with the congregation downstairs. When the minister came out and announced the giving of the peace, one of the gang members spontaneously stood up and yelled, "Hey, dude, you are cool!" The congregation turned around in shock. After the service, the youth worker was told not to bring the gang members back to the church until they learned how to behave *inside* a church.

The church *should* have turned around and invited the gang members downstairs. They should have applauded a woman who was doing an amazing job of evangelism. Instead, the youth worker was fired. Apparently this church was more concerned about comfort than it was about a group of gang members' discomforting search for spirituality.

Seek the spiritual life, admit your messiness, follow Christ wherever he leads you, and discomfort is right around the corner.

A group of us in ministry have been acquainted for years. We meet two or three times a year and share life stories, pray, and worship together. True, we are not the closest of friends, but we know each other very well. Or so we thought. A few months ago, we were sitting around the table catching up when one person set a cassette recorder on the table, announcing he wanted to play a tape for us. It was a recording of a testimony he had given recently at his church. I cannot describe for you the shock on all of our faces as our friend's voice told of a lifelong struggle with alcohol, which he had managed to hide from his wife, his children, and all of us. It took a lot of courage for our friend to share the pain of the years of hiding his addiction.

The silence lasted a long time. Each of us was confronting our own secrets. Each of us was struggling with the shock and the discomfort of realizing we didn't know our friend very well. In fact, we were realizing, we didn't know anyone in our group very well. You could cut the awkwardness with a knife. Of course, our friend sat there petrified that his openness would cause us to reject him, that we would be angry because he hadn't said anything before now, or worse, that we would judge him as unfit to call himself a Christian and would label him phony or untrustworthy.

The Attack of the Name-Callers

When Jesus and his followers show up, it isn't long before people start pointing fingers and calling names. Jesus was called all kinds of names: wine-bibber (what is a wine-bibber, anyway?), Sabbath breaker, blasphemer. Over the centuries, religious people have refined name-calling to an art. The name most commonly used today? *Unspiritual!*

Because our church is a church "for people who don't like to go to church," many of our members have been called names by a church (which is why they don't like to go to church) or by those who attend one.

The body of Christ can be mean.

If a person is trying to follow Christ, and others are concerned about what they are doing or how they are doing it, name-calling can become vicious.

For almost forty years, Margaret had lived with the memory of one soul-scarring day in the one-room schoolhouse she attended. From the first day Margaret came to class, she and Ms. Garner, her bitter and harsh teacher, didn't get along. Over the years, the animosity between them only worsened until one fateful day when she was nine years old, Margaret's life was forever altered.

That day, Margaret frantically raced into her classroom after recess, late again. Ms. Garner was furious. "Margaret!"

she shouted, "we have been waiting for you! Get up here to the front of the class, right now!"

Margaret walked slowly to the teacher's desk, was told to face the class, and then the nightmare began.

Ms. Garner ranted, "Boys and girls, Margaret has been a bad girl. I have tried to help her to be responsible. But, apparently, she doesn't want to learn. So we must teach her a lesson. We must force her to face what a selfish person she has become. I want each of you to come to the front of the room, take a piece of chalk, and write something bad about Margaret on the blackboard. Maybe this experience will motivate her to become a better person!"

Margaret stood frozen next to Ms. Garner. One by one, the students began a silent procession to the blackboard. One by one, the students wrote their life-smothering words, slowly extinguishing the light in Margaret's soul. "Margaret is stupid! Margaret is selfish! Margaret is fat! Margaret is a dummy!" On and on they went, until twenty-five terrible scribblings of Margaret's "badness" screamed from the blackboard.

The venomous sentences taunted Margaret in what felt like the longest day of her life. After walking home with each caustic word indelibly written on her soul, she crawled into her bed, claiming sickness, and tried to cry the pain away, but the pain never left, and forty years later, she slumped in the waiting room of a psychologist's office, still cringing in the shadow of those twenty-five sentences. To her horror, Margaret had slowly become what the students had written.

Margaret's teacher knew exactly what she was doing. She knew the power of name-calling. Margaret was humiliated by a thoughtless and cruel act, robbed of the sparkle in her eye, cursed to live the rest of her life in the shadow of that nightmarish experience.

I believe many of us have experienced Margaret's humiliation.

One day we decided to become a follower of Christ, to seek his presence in our lives, and were doing our best to keep Jesus in our sights when we were shocked to discover our fellow "classmates" calling us names. "Ungodly. Uncommitted. Poor example. Unspiritual. Carnal. Unbiblical." In other words, "You are 'doing God' all wrong."

The Kingdom Monitors and the Condemners

According to his critics, *Jesus* "did God" all wrong. He went to the wrong places, said the wrong things, and worst of all, let just anyone into the kingdom. Jesus scandalized an intimidating, elitist, country-club religion by opening membership in the spiritual life to those who had been denied it. What made people furious was Jesus' "irresponsible" habit of throwing open the doors of his love to the whosoevers, the just-any-ones, and the not-a-chancers like you and me.

Nothing makes people in the church more angry than grace. It's ironic: we stumble into a party we weren't invited to and find the uninvited standing at the door making sure no other uninviteds get in. Then a strange phenomenon occurs: as soon as we are included in the party because of Jesus' irresponsible love, we decide to make grace "more responsible" by becoming self-appointed Kingdom Monitors, guarding the kingdom of God, keeping the riffraff out (which, as I understand it, are who the kingdom of God is supposed to include).

John tells the story of a man like us, an outsider, a blind outsider. The blind man bumped into Jesus, found his blindness "ruined" by him, and became a scandal to the religious leaders of his day. His miraculous encounter with Jesus is a model for all of us who are trying to live spiritual lives.

In chapter 9, we meet this man, who was blind from birth, sitting in his familiar place, begging. The disciples bring up some theological question about whether his blindness was caused by his own sin or by his parents' sin. They are not concerned about the blind *man;* what they are concerned about is the *theology* of blindness. The disciples attempt to have a theological discussion, and Jesus cuts it short. He makes it very clear that what matters is glorifying God, helping blind men and women see. The disciples are worried about theories and doctrines; *Jesus is worried about the blind man.*

In effect, Jesus says, "Your philosophizing about the cause of blindness is interesting, but *wait until you see this!* Talking about God's power is one thing, but look what happens when you are in the presence of his power. A little mud, a little water, and the blind man is no longer blind."

Now the blind man's troubles really begin! Sometimes when blind people get unblind, their closest friends are not happy. Meeting Jesus does not always result in our troubles ending; sometimes our troubles just begin. Jesus warns us, "Do not suppose that I have come to bring peace to the earth. I did not come to bring peace, but a sword." Begin a relationship with Jesus, and we're going to get in the same kind of trouble Jesus did.

When the man who was formerly blind returns to his neighborhood, his neighbors refuse to believe he can see. Afraid of mystery, unable to fathom the possibility of a miracle, the neighbors turn their backs on their friend and drag him to those who should have known something about mystery, miracle, and spirituality—the religious leaders, the Condemners. The sabotage of the blind man begins.

How should you and I respond to intimidation? How can we survive when those around us criticize our spirituality or, worse, reject us because we're not religious enough? The blind man gives us some clues.

Living Our "Ignorance"

The Pharisees, the theologians of the day, the Kingdom Monitors, who know Scripture like the backs of their hands (instead of knowing it in the fronts of their hearts), should have been ready to celebrate. Instead, they are ready to condemn.

"Tell us, Mr. Blind Man, how did you get your eyesight back?"

The man's answer is very bizarre. "A stranger made mud with his own spit, stuck it in my eyes, and ordered me to wash it off in the Pool of Siloam. I did what he said. Now I can see."

The blind man flunks Religion 101.

The Kingdom Monitors know more about God than an uneducated, uncouth blind man, or so they believe. A heated lecture ensues.

"Any Sunday school student knows that people who are blind from birth are paying for the sins of their family. The real God doesn't use mud to heal people, especially from self-appointed prophets no one has heard of. And most certainly, *God doesn't heal on the Sabbath.*"

Religious people love to hide behind religion. They love the rules of religion more than they love Jesus. With practice, Condemners let rules become more important than the spiritual life.

John Mackie was the president of the Church of Scotland after World War II. With two other ministers from a rather severe and pietistic denomination, he traveled to remote parts of the Balkan Peninsula to check on missionaries they supported.

The three clergymen called on an Orthodox priest in a small Greek village. Excited to see the visitors, the priest offered the clergymen a glass of rare and expensive wine. Horrified, the two pietistic ministers refused. Dr. Mackie, on the other hand, took a glassful, sniffed it like a wine connoisseur, sipped it, and praised its quality. He even asked for another glass. His companions were noticeably upset by Dr. Mackie's behavior.

Later, when the three men were in the jeep again, making their way up the rough road out of the village, the two pious clergymen turned on Dr. Mackie.

"Dr. Mackie," they said, "do you mean to tell us that you are the president of the Church of Scotland and an officer of the World Council of Churches and you drink?"

Dr. Mackie had had all he could take, and his Scottish temper got the better of him. "No, I don't," he said, "but *somebody* had to be a Christian!"[3]

My hunch is Dr. Mackie didn't convince his condemners. The rules of their faith were much more important than showing grace. They were much more excited about condemning the faith of Dr. Mackie and the priest than they were about living their own faith.

The Condemners try to force the blind man to renounce Jesus by asking him to confirm that Jesus is anything but the Messiah, that in fact he is a sinner.

What can the blind man possibly say to defend himself?

He trusts his ignorance.

He says, "Whether he is a sinner or not, I don't know. One thing I do know. *I was blind but now I see!*" The blind man does the only thing he can; he tells his strange, contradictory, politically incorrect, irrational story. He tells the truth—the sum of his theological training—which, by the way, is where all good theology starts: with the truth.

Brennan Manning tells the story of a recent convert to Jesus who was approached by an unbelieving friend.

"So you have been converted to Christ?"

"Yes."

"Then you must know a great deal about Him. Tell me, what country was he born in?"

"I don't know."

"What was his age when he died?"

"I don't know."

"How many sermons did he preach?"

"I don't know."

"You certainly know very little for a man who claims to be converted to Christ."

"You are right. I am ashamed at how little I know about Him. But this much I know: Three years ago I was a drunkard. I was in debt. My family was falling to pieces; they dreaded the sight of me. But now I have given up drink. We are out of debt. Ours is a happy home. My children eagerly await my return home each evening. All this Christ has done for me. This much I know of Christ!"[4]

Maybe the alcoholic and the blind man didn't know much about Jesus, but they knew plenty about their *encounters* with Jesus. The alcoholic and the blind man may not have studied biblical history, but their lives had been changed by the truth, and the Pharisees (then and now) knew it.

Armed with their superior education, their flawless theology, and the power of their religion, the Pharisees desperately try to regain control by attacking with questions. "Is Jesus of the devil? Where is he? What do you know about him?"

The blind man knows very little about Jesus, but he is an expert in first-time seeing. He doesn't know where Jesus is, but he knows what Jesus did. He can't define a messiah, but he certainly can describe what it is like to see a flower for the first time. When confronted with questions about Jesus, the blind man is not afraid to say, "I don't know."

"I don't know" is often the only reply we can give to explain the mystery of Christ.

Jesus often left his followers "I don't know-ing." Our personal relationship with Christ is often the only apologetic we can offer. Our lack of knowing is the beginning of humility and the very essence of the spiritual life.

The Intimidated Becomes the Intimidator

Dragged before his neighbors, his family, and the Pharisees, the blind man is pummeled by all of them. His neighbors don't believe him, his parents abandon him, and the Pharisees attack him physically as well as emotionally. They try to intimidate him, to shut him up.

But the blind man will not shut up. Apparently, a few minutes *with* Jesus teaches us more about God than a lifetime of studying *about* God. (Trust your relationship with Jesus!) And then, without warning, the lectured *to* becomes the lectur*er*.

"What's the matter with you guys? You don't know who this man is, yet he opened my eyes on command? God doesn't listen to sinners, yet he listened to this man? Hmmm. Makes me think he must be from God, because if he weren't, how could he have done what he just did?"

The Pharisees are so enraged they physically throw the blind man out of the synagogue, leaving him alone. Telling the truth can get you killed . . . or, at the least, beat up.

And here is the biggest tragedy of all. Not one person in the entire ninth chapter of John, including the blind man's parents, do what any follower of Christ should have done: *throw a party!* When a man or woman has just received their sight after a lifetime of blindness, someone should order the wine, start the music, and *begin the celebration!* The spiritual life is not just about rules and regulations, teaching and theology, lectures and sermons. Life with Jesus is meant to be lived, not smothered, dissected, inspected, or condemned. The blind man should have had the time of his life! His moment of healing should have been commemorated as a moment he would never forget.

One of my son's friends (I'll call him Greg) recently celebrated his twenty-eighth birthday. Greg's parents were not happy with his life choices, especially his decision to live with his girlfriend, Diane. Knowing his parents' displeasure, Greg and Diane decided to get married, and they called his parents to give them the good news. "We want to be married in Minnesota, so the entire family can come." Greg's parents were happy but restrained.

While they were planning the wedding, Diane discovered she was pregnant. Realizing the pregnancy would upset his parents, Greg decided to call off the wedding and use the money they were going to spend on it for their baby instead. Greg and Diane opted for a courthouse wedding with a justice of the peace presiding. Only my son and his girlfriend witnessed the union.

A couple of weeks later, my son and his girlfriend were with some friends, and the subject of Greg's wedding came up. Everyone concluded that it was more like a nonwedding— impersonal and isolated. As they talked, their conviction grew. No wedding should be an impersonal, isolated, bureaucratic legal transaction. Weddings should be celebrated. The couple should be surrounded with the support and care of family and friends. The group looked at each other and almost in unison said, "Why don't we give Greg and Diane the wedding they never had?" As soon as the words left their mouths, they knew what had to be done. Even though Greg and Diane were legally married, the group decided to gift them with a "real" wedding. The date was set, both families were called, and surprisingly, they all agreed to come to the surprise wedding. Sixty friends and family were involved in a conspiracy of grace.

To ensure that the couple was available on their new wedding day, Greg and Diane were invited to my son's home for a "dress up" dinner. When they arrived, a group of their friends kidnapped them separately and each was given the bachelor and bachelorette party they'd never had. The bride and groom were separately driven to a secluded place where, seated in a circle with their same-gender friends, they were asked a series of questions like, "Now that you have been married for three months, what mistakes have you made? How can we help you in your marriage?" Both the young husband and wife were given a picture of their spouse and asked to write on the back all the reasons they loved that person.

When the parties were finished, Greg and Diane thought that the surprise was over. You can imagine their shock when they were returned to the house, only to discover sixty of their family and friends waiting for them, laughing and yelling, "Surprise!" The hugging and the crying began. It took Greg and Diane a long time to stop crying, and after they regained their composure, the entire group moved to the back yard surrounded with flowers, where a minister was waiting. The couple exchanged vows, each parent vowed their support, and each friend walked by and whispered a blessing to Greg and Diane. When the service was completed, there wasn't a dry eye anywhere. Everyone left knowing they had participated in a moment of grace. This wedding had "Jesus" written all over it.

The Kingdom Monitors would raise their voices immediately. "You can't do this! You are condoning the sins of two young people who lived together and conceived a baby before they were married. Real Christians do not condone unbiblical living!" And they would be correct. Christians do not *condone* unbiblical living; we *redeem* it. Greg and Diane were able to glimpse redemption in one grace-filled experience.

Jesus Rights the Wrongs

At the end of the blind man's story are these words: "Jesus heard that they had thrown him [the blind man] out, and when he had *found* him . . ." Jesus did not forget the blind man. He did not abandon him but sought him out, came after him, found him—"wrong" answers, "wrong" explanations, "wrong" theology and all. Jesus finds you and me and says, I think, the same thing he said to a woman who faced the condemnation of everyone around her: "Has no one condemned you? *Then neither do I condemn you!*"[5]

Remember Margaret? After decades of depression and anxiety, she had finally sought help and was having the last meeting with her psychologist. Two long years of weekly counseling helped Margaret to finally extricate herself from her past. It had been a long and difficult road, but she smiled at her counselor (how long it had been since she'd smiled!) as they talked about her readiness to move on.

"Well, Margaret," the counselor said softly, "I guess it's graduation day for you. How are you feeling?"

After a long silence, Margaret spoke. "I . . . I'm okay."

The counselor hesitated. "Margaret, I know this will be difficult, but just to make sure you're ready to move on, I am going to ask you to do something. I want to go back to your schoolroom and detail the events of that day. Take your time. Describe each of the children as they approach the blackboard, remember what they wrote and how you felt—all twenty-five students."

In a way, this would be easy for Margaret. For forty years she had remembered every detail. And yet, to go through the nightmare one more time would take every bit of strength she had. After a long silence, she began the painful description. One by one, she described each of the students vividly, as though she had just seen them, stopping periodically to regain her composure, forcing herself to face each of those students one more time.

Finally, she was done, and the tears would not stop, could not stop. Margaret cried a long time before she realized someone was whispering her name. "Margaret. Margaret. Margaret." She looked up to see her counselor staring into her eyes, saying her name over and over again. Margaret stopped crying for a moment.

"Margaret. You . . . you left out one person."

"I certainly did *not!* I have lived with this story for forty years. I know every student by heart."

"No, Margaret, you did forget someone. See, he's sitting in the back of the classroom. He's standing up, walking toward your teacher, Ms. Garner. She is handing him a piece of chalk and he's taking it, Margaret, he's taking it! Now he's walking over to the blackboard and picking up an eraser. *He is erasing every one of the sentences the students wrote.* They are gone! Margaret, they are gone! Now he's turning and looking at you, Margaret. Do you recognize him yet? Yes, his name is Jesus. Look, he's writing new sentences on the board. 'Margaret is loved. Margaret is beautiful. Margaret is gentle and kind. Margaret is strong. Margaret has great courage.'"

And Margaret began to weep. But very quickly, the weeping turned into a smile, and then into laughter, and then into tears of joy.[6]

After forty dark years, Margaret was no longer condemned, no longer alone, and no longer rejected. The blindness of her past horror was removed. Margaret and a certain blind man—and maybe even you and me—can shout with confidence, "Once I was blind, but now I see!"

4

the ugliness of rejection
Paralyzed by Our Past

How unutterably sweet is the knowledge that our Heavenly Father knows us completely. No talebearer can inform on us; no enemy can make an accusation stick; no forgotten skeleton can come tumbling out of some hidden closet to abash us and expose our past; no unsuspected weakness in our characters can come to light to turn God away from us, since He knew us utterly before we knew him and called us to Himself in the full knowledge of everything that was against us.

A. W. TOZER, *THE KNOWLEDGE OF THE HOLY*

From one religious camp we're told that what God wants is obedience, or sacrifice, or adherence to the right doctrines, or morality. Those are the answers offered by conservative churches. The more therapeutic churches suggest that no, God is after our contentment, or happiness, or self-actualization, or

> *something else along those lines. He is concerned*
> *about all these things, of course, but they are not his*
> *primary concern. What he is after is us—our laugh-*
> *ter, our dreams, our fears, our heart of hearts.*
> Brent Curtis and John Eldredge, *Sacred Romance*

I'm a minister."

"Oh, really? Where did you attend seminary?"

"Uh . . . I didn't go to seminary."

"Bible college?"

"No."

"Are you ordained?"

"Well . . . uh . . . not exactly."

I could see the looks on their faces, and I could hear what they were thinking. *You're not ordained? No Bible training and you pastor this church? What kind of flaky, illegitimate, Mickey Mouse church is this?* And I was thinking to myself, *Why didn't I go to seminary? I should have taken college more seriously. Man, did I screw up my past.*

Rejection. The paralyzing experience of disapproval, repudiation, exclusion, ostracism. Religion has been good at rejection. Rejection keeps us at arm's length and stamps us with the label "loser." Which should be good news for you and me because, guess what? Jesus is attracted to losers. Jesus' losers are great candidates for spirituality.

The Spirituality of Losers

Talk about a loser.

Talk about a moral disaster.

Talk about a person who has made too many mistakes, failed too many times.

Talk about a woman who is a mess. The Samaritan woman in the fourth chapter of John gives new meaning to the word *mess.*

When it comes to immorality, this woman is a pro. Of all the people to bump into the Son of God, it had to be a woman whose past suggests she is as far from God as anyone could be. Surprisingly, Jesus initiates a conversation with her. A respectable Jewish male (especially a respectable Jewish Messiah male) should not be talking to a woman like her, period. A woman with her reputation could only damage Jesus' reputation, *but he doesn't seem to care!*

Strangely, this woman has studied religion. She knows messiahs, and divorced five times, she definitely knows men, but she's never met a man or a Messiah like this one. This *man* treats her with respect. What kind of a man is he? He listens to her, dialogues with her, takes her questions seriously, and treats her with dignity and kindness. *Thank God,* she thinks, *he doesn't know what kind of woman I am.*

But he *does* know what kind of woman she is.

Turns out *she* doesn't know what kind of woman she is. Jesus brings her face to face with herself. She would do anything to avoid facing who she has become. Jesus knows she can't pretend her sin away; she has to face it, look at it, admit it. Jesus knows that in order to get well, she has to get real!

Jesus doesn't lecture, condemn, or humiliate; instead, he gently reminds the woman where her choices have led her. Standing at this unlikely place, her past and her reputation no longer a secret, she admits her deepest longing—her longing for the Messiah. Now she can admit that in her futile search for relationships, she really had been looking for water—living water. In her lifetime of fumbling around for the right man, what she really had been fumbling around for was God. And now he stands before her.

Rather than focusing on her mistakes, Jesus focuses on *her desire for God*. Jesus recognizes her lifetime search for love in all the wrong places and honors her unsavory past by looking into her heart. Jesus leads her to himself.

This woman has truly messed up her life, and Jesus meets her in the middle of her mess. No wonder she drops her bucket and runs into town screaming, "Come see a man who told me everything I've ever done!"

Ashamed of her past? Not anymore. All she can think about is her future. A woman whose past has defined her is now defined by her present. Her muddled, mistake-ridden, sin-cluttered past has driven her to a man like no other man, and she wants everyone to meet him.

When Jesus Meets Our Past

All of the cards are stacked against the woman at the well. Looking at her long string of bad choices, many would consider her unredeemable, unsalvageable, unteachable, and beyond help. She hasn't just made a few mistakes; she has lived a lifetime of mistakes, enough to cause most to conclude her life is scarred beyond hope. She comes to the well at the middle of the day because respectable women come in the morning, and she understands that she is no respectable woman.

But Jesus respects her.

Jesus doesn't see what everyone else sees.

As far as Jesus is concerned, this woman is salvageable, teachable, and redeemable. As far as Jesus is concerned, the woman with no future has a future; the woman with a string of failures is about to have the string broken. Jesus sees her present desire, which makes her past irrelevant.

You don't suppose, do you, the same could be true for you and me? Our mistakes, our strings of failures, and what everyone else labels unredeemable may actually *be* redeemable? You don't suppose the mess we've made of our lives can be the place where we meet Jesus? Do you?

Our Past Is a Reflection of Our Longings

Our search for love, for meaning, for happiness, is often our search for God in disguise. When the bottom falls out of our lives, when we come to a dead end, when there is no place to go, we often get in touch with our longings for God. Religion had told the Samaritan woman about the possibility of a Messiah, and she meets the real Messiah, who immediately recognizes her thirst and offers her the living water of his grace. What this woman expects from the Messiah is a lengthy critique, an enlightening lecture on what she should do, a harsh and justifiable reminder of the consequences of her destructive choices on others. What she receives instead is compassion, gentleness, kindness, and a way out of the ruins of her life.

Jesus goes straight for her longings, finds them, and in the process finds *her.*

In a book by New Zealand author Mike Riddell, Vincent has met and fallen in love with a young girl named Marilyn. Neither one of them is seeking a relationship, but a relationship is seeking them. Swept up by their emotions, the two become deeply involved. Marilyn, a prostitute, is not prepared to fall in love and is certainly not prepared for the honesty love requires. She must tell Vincent who she is, knowing full well that her painful disclosure will probably mean the end of their relationship.

"Vincent?"
"Mmmm."

"There's ah . . . there's something we need to talk about."

"Only if you want to. I'm happy just to sit here and look at you. Sorry, this looks like something serious." Looks a lot like the intro to the Dear John speech, truth be told.

"It's about me and what I do."

"Yeah, I wondered when you were going to pluck up the courage to talk about it. Don't tell me, you work for the CIA, right? Sorry, sorry, I'll shut up."

She is totally absorbed in the remains of her salad, scrutinizing it for something. Anything to avoid his eyes.

"There's no easy way of saying this. I'm a prostitute. I sleep with men for my living. It's a business. I'm very professional."

Time and silence have this thing they do together. They make a chasm that has no bottom to it. And there you are, standing right on the edge of it. Aware that at any moment you may be falling and falling and falling, with no hope of recovery. At the moment they are at either side of it, each consumed by their private terror. She looks up at last from her salad. Vincent is crying. The tears are streaming down his cheeks, and he is biting his lip to stop himself sobbing.

"I'm sorry. I didn't mean to deceive you. I'm sorry, Vincent. I'm sorry."

He can't speak. He wants to, but nothing is working. He is looking at her, at her beautiful face, at her eyes, at the slight hardness around her mouth. And weeping and weeping. She reaches a hand across to hold his. She is beyond tears, empty and bleak and barren. Vincent is mumbling something, but is incoherent through the pain. And then he begins to repeat it again and again.

"I love you, I love you, I love you, I love you . . ."

This is the worst thing she has ever heard in her life. She wants to scream, to break something, to tip over the table in rage. Instead some continental shelf rips loose within her. She begins gulping and moaning, a terrible agonizing cry from another place. And the tears are flowing. They grip each other's hands, and lean their foreheads together. The tears are flowing into the abyss, and there is no end to them.[1]

Marilyn expected Vincent to reject her, to pull away from her, to have nothing to do with her. In a strange and touching way, Vincent did what Jesus would do; he looked beneath her behavior, saw her longings, and all he could do was weep. She expected criticism; what she received was *understanding.* Instead of hearing words of condemnation, Marilyn heard over and over again, "I love you."

The Ugliness of Rejection

Based on their experiences with religion, both Marilyn and the woman at the well were prepared for cold, recriminating judgment and condemnation. Neither one of them was happy with their life choices; neither needed to be reminded what they had done wrong; neither would have been helped by rubbing salt in their wounds. What they desperately needed, what they desperately wanted, was for someone to recognize what they were *looking for,* not what they were doing. Notice, I did not say they wanted to be legitimized. They weren't looking for someone to condone what they had done; they were looking for someone to accept them. What normally happens to notorious sinners is rejection, distance, separation, and withdrawal. Most people don't like sinners, don't want to be around them, and whether they recognize it or not, make their disdain for the sinner very clear.

One Sunday morning, an older man showed up in our church and sat in the front row. His braided and partially dreadlocked hair hung below his belt; his extremely long frizzy goatee shot in all directions from his chin. His nervousness was obvious. I could feel his fear. When it came time for the welcome, I talked about how important it is for the church to be a place where a few somebodies and mostly nobodies feel safe, no matter how unsafe it is outside the church. When we stood for the giving of the peace, this man mingled throughout our small congregation. After the service, he came up to me, his eyes moist, and said, "I've never been to a church like this. To be honest, I was seriously apprehensive when you announced the giving of the peace. I expected the worst. Do you know what it is like to walk into a church and not one person talks to you, not one person touches you, and no one even acknowledges your presence? I do. You can cut the rejection with a knife. You cannot imagine how alone you feel."

Without knowing it, he had described the woman at the well. She came to the well *alone*. No one wanted to acknowledge her. The visitor to our church was shocked to have been touched, hugged, talked to, acknowledged. It made a deep imprint on him. Which is exactly what happened to the woman at the well.

It is tragic that many of us are afraid to pursue our desire for God because when we have made mistakes and the scars of our choices were visible, others have been quick to isolate us, to distance themselves from us, to question our sincerity and our commitment to change.

The Power of the Unchanged Life

After her conversation with Jesus, the woman at the well is just beginning a whole new way of living, *but none of the facts of her life have changed.* She is still living with a man who isn't her husband. She has still been divorced five times. Her reputation is still a disaster. Jesus often told people not to talk about their encounters with him, but not this woman. Her faith is only a few minutes old and already she has become an evangelist, already she is having a huge influence on her community. What does she say? Not much. "Uh . . . come see a man who told me everything I've ever done." Everyone in town knows what this woman has done. Big deal. What she says is *under*whelming. But the fact that she publicly talks about her shameful past is *over*whelming.

Her words are few and seemingly insignificant, but her saying them at all is very significant. In effect she says, "I know you know who I am, but I just met someone who liberated me from my past, from my reputation, and I am no longer the person you think I am. I am no longer a hostage to my bad choices. I am *free*. I am free." Still, nothing has changed. But *everything* has changed. Her neighbors can hear it in her voice and see it in her eyes. Her words are all they need to race to the man she describes. For reasons they don't understand, who this woman is *now* seems more relevant than who she was *then*.

The implications for us are overwhelming. Those of us who want to move on from our past, those who have come to the end of the road, can start with our *un*changed life, now. We don't have to wait until we are "mature." We don't have to move to a new town or convince others we are serious; we simply start. We begin. We take the first bumbling, stumbling, teetering steps toward the spiritual life, *even if we're not very good at it.*

Little League baseball can be a brutal sport, especially for nine- and ten-year-olds who compete in national tournaments. It was the area Little League championship game. The stands were packed with families of each of the players. One young man brought his mother and father, both grandparents, and three uncles and aunts to watch him play.

The bottom of the seventh inning was a nail-biter. The other team was ahead by one run, the bases were loaded, two outs, and the little boy with the large family was up to bat. If he made an out, the game would be over and his team would lose. If he walked or hit the ball, he would be the hero of the game.

He swung at the first pitch and missed.

"Strike one!" the umpire yelled.

The families from the other team cheered, but his family cheered even louder. "It's okay, Carl. No problem. You almost hit the ball! Now, clobber the next pitch!"

"Strike twooo!" the umpire yelled after the next pitch.

Pandemonium broke out. Both teams and their families were yelling back and forth at each other. Carl's family and team were encouraging him; the players and family of the defensive team were taunting. No one could hear themselves think.

Wrinkles appeared on the nine-year-old's forehead as he waited for the next pitch. As the ball left the pitcher's hand, it became very quiet. The ball sped toward Carl. It seemed like it took forever to cross the plate, but cross the plate it did, and Carl swung with all his might.

"Strike three! You're out!"

Not only was Carl out, the game was over. And he was the cause of the loss.

The winning team went crazy, their families swarmed onto the field, and everyone was dancing, laughing, cheering, and celebrating. Except Carl's team. As Carl's team walked off the field, dejected, they mingled with their families and headed back to their cars in silence.

Except for Carl.

Carl was still standing at the plate, devastated, alone, his head down in disgrace.

Suddenly someone yelled, "Okay, Carl, play ball!" Startled, Carl looked up to see his family spread out over the field. Grandpa was pitching, Dad was catching, Mom was at first base, Uncle David was at second, and the rest of the family had covered the other positions.

"Come on, Carl, pick up the bat. Grandpa's pitching."

Bewildered, Carl slowly picked up the bat and swung at Grandpa's first pitch. He missed, and he missed the next six pitches as well. But on the seventh pitch, determined to get a hit, Carl smacked the ball to left field. His aunt ran, picked up the ball, and threw it to first base in plenty of time, but the first baseman, Mom, must have lost the ball in the sun, because it went right through her hands into the dugout. "Run!" everyone yelled. As Carl was running to second, the first baseman recovered the ball and threw it. Amazingly, Uncle David was blinded by the sun as well. "Keep running!" yelled someone, and Carl headed for third, where the throw went at least two feet over the head of the third baseman. "Keep running, Carl!" and Carl raced for home, running as hard as he had ever run. The ball was thrown with deadly accuracy as the catcher, blocking home plate, waited to tag him out, but just as Carl reached home plate, the ball bounced in and out of the catcher's mitt, and Carl was safe!

Before he knew what happened, Carl found himself being carried around on Uncle David's shoulders while the rest of the family crowded around cheering Carl's name.

One person who was watching this amazing event commented to a friend, "I watched a little boy fall victim to a *conspiracy of grace!*"

Carl, the loser—the one who struck out, failed his team, disappointed his family—went from loser to hero. Carl, who would have been left with the awful memory of his failure, was instead given a memory of grace, love, and acceptance.

Just like a certain woman at a well.

I know about conspiracies of grace. I have been the victim of one myself.

My lack of training as a minister, my unordained status, if I'm honest, has bothered me as much as it bothers others. My uneducated past haunts me.

Two years ago, I was invited to speak for the Oregon Seventh Day Adventists annual ministers' retreat. Over one hundred and fifty ministers from the state of Oregon attended. I am not a Seventh Day Adventist, but I have always considered Adventists brothers and sisters in Christ, even though I disagree with some of their doctrines. I was invited to speak about the need for youth ministry, allowing both the Adventists and myself to relax about any differences we might have.

In the process of talking about youth, I found myself talking about the frustrations of the pastorate and noticed how many of the ministers were resonating with my thoughts about the church. Midway through my talks, I abandoned my youth ministry remarks and talked about the loneliness and struggles of the pastorate. I referred many times to my lack of ordination, and yet I noticed how well we connected, even to the point of tears for some of the ministers.

After I had finished my final talk, the leaders came forward and asked me to stay. They had a gift for me. I had a good idea what my gift would be—a T-shirt (which is the gift of choice for most conferences). Was I wrong.

The state director said, "Mike, you have spent the entire weekend apologizing for your lack of training. You have constantly referred to yourself as a 'K-Mart minister' and reminded us you aren't a real minister because you aren't ordained. Well, you are wrong, Mike, because you have ministered to us this week. We think you are a real minister. While you've been speaking, we've been in contact with our national headquarters, and as far as we know, this has never been done before, but we want to ordain you in the Seventh Day Adventist Church!"

The entire room sat in stunned silence. People looked shocked at first, then hesitant, and suddenly everyone was walking toward the front of the room. One hundred and fifty ministers laid hands on me and ordained me. After the service, none of us knew how to respond or how to explain what had just happened.

But I knew what had happened. Jesus was in the building. I think Jesus was tired of my whining, tired of hearing me question my calling, so he decided to shut me up for good. I could just see him smiling. "Okay, are you happy? Now you are ordained, so shut up already." Of course, I went back to my church and told them I had good news and bad news. I was now ordained, but we were meeting on Saturdays.

Jesus can redeem our past, no matter what kind of past we bring with us: failure, mistakes, bad decisions, immaturity, and even a past which was done to us.

The Freedom of the Present

Not everyone has chosen their past. Too many carry the scars of physical, mental, or psychological abuse, awakening each day to the haunting memories of a time when they were acted upon, against their will, and now find themselves hopelessly trapped between facing their past or running from it. A sad reality of modern life is the increasing number of people whose past abuse has convinced them of their unworthiness.

Often it is the abused who have decided they are disqualified from the possibility of God's grace. The abused see themselves as damaged beyond repair, soiled goods which cannot be cleaned, prisoners who cannot be freed.

Evangelist Rich Wilkerson once held a large crusade in Washington state. Many hundreds came forward that night, too many for Rich to meet individually. A few weeks after the crusade, he received a letter from a young college girl:

Dear Mr. Wilkerson,

I attended your crusade in Seattle a few weeks ago. It's my first year of college and a group of my friends invited me to come to your crusade. I agreed, reluctantly, but I was desperate. The preceeding four years before college were the worst years of my life and I was willing to try anything that might help. My nightmare started when I turned fourteen. That was the year my uncle moved into our home. Shortly after he moved in, he would sneak into my bedroom and sexually abuse me. He threatened to hurt me if I told anyone, so I endured the abuse, saying nothing, anxiously awaiting my first year of college when I would be out of the house.

By the time I entered college, I was a mess. My first year was a disaster. I slept with any guy who would have me, drank and drugged myself into forgetfulness almost every night, but I would still be awakened by nightmares. When I came to your crusade, I was at the breaking point, and when you asked us to come forward to meet Jesus, I almost ran to the front.

On the five hour drive home, I fell asleep. I dreamed I was asleep in my college dorm room when I was awakened by my uncle once again. I wanted to scream for help or get out of bed and run, but I could do neither. He kept asking me to come to him, and I could not resist. I could feel myself giving up and coming to him once again, when suddenly the door to my dorm room opened again. It was Jesus with his arms wide open, beckoning me to come to him. I jumped out of bed and ran past my uncle into the arms of Jesus. I woke up with all the girls in the car looking at me because I was crying, saying out loud, "I'm free! I'm free! I'm really free."[2]

A young college girl with a past meets the Jesus of the present. As with the woman at the well, nothing had changed and everything had changed. Abuse was still part of her past, but hope was now part of her present. I can see her saying to her friends, "Come see a man who liberated me from my past." As messy as this woman's past had been, she was now free to seek the spiritual life.

5

odd discipleship
The Consequence of a Lopsided Spirituality

Vocation does not mean a goal that I pursue. It means a calling that I hear. Before I can tell my life what I want to do with it, I must listen to my life telling me who I am.

PARKER PALMER, *LET YOUR LIFE SPEAK*

When artists discover as children that they have inappropriate responses to events around them, they also find, as they learn to trust those responses, that these oddities are what constitute their value to others.

KATHLEEN NORRIS, *THE CLOISTER WALK*

He got all "A's" and flunked life.

WALKER PERCY

It is not going to be easy to listen to God's call. Your insecurity, your self-doubt, and your great need for affirmation make you lose trust in your inner voice

*and run away from yourself. But you know that God
speaks to you through your inner voice and that you
will find joy and peace only if you follow it.*

HENRI NOUWEN, *THE INNER VOICE OF LOVE*

One of my favorite stories is about a boy named Norman in Robert Fulghum's book *Uh-Oh.*

Remember in elementary school when the teacher would announce the spring play? Every student's hand would shoot into the air volunteering to be one of the characters. Of course, the choice characters would be handed out first. In Fulghum's book, Norman's teacher announced the play for the year—*Cinderella.* Chaos ensued as a sea of arms waved wildly, each student trying to get the teacher's attention. "I want to be Cinderella!" every girl yelled. "I want to be the handsome prince!" the boys shouted. Realizing that not everyone could have the same part, the students soon erupted into urgent requests for other parts. "I want to be the wicked stepmother!" "I want to be an ugly stepsister!" Somehow the teacher was able to wade through all the requests, and soon everyone was assigned a part.

Except for Norman. Norman was a quiet young man who didn't talk much in class. He wasn't shy or bashful; he just didn't feel like talking a lot of the time. Talking about nothing was a waste of time to Norman; he talked only when he had something to say. Norman had a mind of his own and was perfectly comfortable just being himself.

Concerned because there weren't any characters left (even though she had made up many extra parts) and knowing Norman very well, the teacher said, "Norman, I'm afraid all the main parts have been taken for *Cinderella.* I'm sure we can find an extra part for you. What character would you like to be?"

Norman didn't hesitate. "I would like to be the pig," he declared.

"Pig?" the teacher said, bewildered. "But there is no pig in *Cinderella*."

Norman smiled and said, "There is now."

Norman designed his own costume—paper cup for a nose and pink long underwear with a pipe-cleaner tail. Norman's pig followed Cinderella wherever she went and became a mirror of the action on stage. If Cinderella was happy, the pig was happy; if Cinderella was sad, the pig was sad. One look at Norman and you knew the emotion of the moment. At the end of the play, when the handsome prince placed the glass slipper on Cinderella's foot and the couple hugged and ran off happily together,

> Norman went wild with joy, danced around on his hind legs, and broke his silence by barking. In rehearsal, the teacher had tried explaining to Norman that even if there was a pig in Cinderella, pigs don't bark. But as she expected, Norman explained that *this* pig barked. And the barking, she had to admit, *was* well done. The presentation at the teachers' conference was a smash hit. At the curtain call, guess who received a standing ovation? Of course, Norman the barking pig. Who was, after all, the *real* Cinderella story.[1]

What I love about the story is Norman's stubbornness. Impervious to intimidation, resisting the limits of the script, Norman refused to believe he had no place. Rather than the script limiting Norman, Norman found a way to enhance the script, to fill it full of life and laughter and surprise.

Norman was so like Jesus. The religious leaders of the day had written the script for the Messiah. When Jesus announced *he* was the Messiah, the Pharisees and others screamed at him,

"There is no Jesus in the Messiah script. Messiahs do not hang out with losers. Our Messiah does not break all rules. Our Messiah does not question our leadership or threaten our religion or act so irresponsibly. Our Messiah does not disregard his reputation, befriend riffraff, or frequent the haunts of questionable people."

Jesus' reply? *"This* Messiah does"!

Do you see why Christianity is called "good news"? Christianity proclaims that it is an equal-opportunity faith, open to all, in spite of the abundance of playwrights in the church who are more than anxious to announce, "There is no place for you in Christianity if you [wear an earring/have a tattoo/drink wine/have too many questions/look weird/ smoke/dance/haven't been filled with the Spirit/aren't baptized/swear/have pink hair/are in the wrong ethnic group/ have a nose ring/have had an abortion/are gay or lesbian/are too conservative or too liberal]."

Jesus believed that messiahs find places for those who have *no* place, and as a result, he invited every Norman he could find—from sleazy businessmen, terrorists, dockworkers, bully tax collectors, psychotics, and hopelessly deranged outcasts, to the successful, rich, and overprivileged elite of society. The Christianity of Jesus became the "place maker" for those who had no place.

The Gift of Oddness

What characterizes Christianity in the modern world is its oddness. Christianity is home for people who are out of step, unfashionable, unconventional, and countercultural. As Peter says, "strangers and aliens."

Churches are not glistening cathedrals filled exclusively with beautiful Cinderellas. Churches are noisy, rollicking madhouses filled with yelping, dancing, barking pigs who follow the *real* Cinderella wherever he goes. Churches are not only awe inspiring; they are *odd* inspiring, attracting an earthy assortment of Jesus' followers. The stained glass is extraordinary, but it is also covered with ordinary fingerprints. Dirt from the fields is scattered on the glistening marble sanctuary floors. Hanging in the air throughout the cathedral of Christ is the heavenly smell of incense mingled with the piggy fragrance of sweaty, commonplace messy disciples.

I pastor the slowest growing church in America. We started twelve years ago with ninety members and have ungrown to thirty. We are about as far as you can get from a user-friendly church—not because our congregation is unfriendly but because our services are unpredictable, unpolished, and inconsistent. We are an "odd friendly" church, attracting unique and different followers of Christ who make every service a surprise.

One Sunday morning, one of our parishioners forgot she was to read the Scripture. When it was time for the reading, there was a long, awkward silence. Conscious that something was awry, the woman looked up and realized everyone was staring at her. Shocked at her lapse of memory, she blurted out a . . . er . . . very "colorful" word. Another long silence followed, and then the laughter began. It was the strangest call to the reading of the gospel I have ever experienced. The woman was embarrassed, apologized, and went on to read the Scripture. I am certainly not condoning the use of swear words in church, but it *was* an accident, it *was* funny, and we had to admit, she read the Scripture with a humility and a vigor that our church hadn't seen in years.

Such happenings are not unusual in our church because we refuse to edit oddness and incompetence from our services. We believe our oddness matters. We want our services filled with mistakes and surprises, because life is full of mistakes and surprises.

One Sunday morning, during the time for prayer requests, a member began describing her father's critical illness. Because she was close to her father, her request for prayer was frequently interrupted by tears. Those around her reached out a hand or nodded with sadness. Some found their eyes filling with tears. The woman finished her request as best as she could. Seated in the front row was Sadie. Sadie stood and walked up the aisle until she saw the woman in the middle of her row. Stepping over the feet of other people in the aisle, Sadie reached the woman, bent down on her knees, laid her head on the woman's lap, and cried with her. Sadie inconvenienced an entire row of people, stepped on their shoes, and forced them to make room for her, but none of us will ever forget that moment. Sadie is *still* teaching the rest of us what the odd compassion of Christ's church looks like.

Odd versus Same

Someone once said, "You shall know the truth, and the truth shall make you odd." Whoever made that statement understood what it means to be a follower of Christ. Followers of Christ are odd. Oddness is important because it is the quality that adds color, texture, variety, beauty to the human condition. Christ doesn't make us the same. What he does is *affirm our differentness*. Oddness is important because the most dangerous word in Western culture is *sameness*. Sameness is a virus that infects members of industrialized nations and causes an allergic reaction to anyone who is different. This virus affects the decision-making part of our brains, resulting in an obsession with making the identical choices everyone else is making.

Sameness is a disease with disasterous consequences—differences are ignored, uniqueness is not listened to, our gifts are cancelled out. Life, passion, and joy are snuffed out. Sameness is the result of sin and does much more than infect us with lust and greed; it flattens the human race, franchises us, attempts to make us all homogenous. Sameness is the cemetery where our distinctiveness is buried. In a sea of sameness, no one has an identity. But Christians do have an identity. We're aliens! We are the odd ones, the strange ones, the misfits, the outsiders, the incompatibles. Oddness is a gift from God and sits dormant until God's Spirit gives it life and shape. Oddness is the consequence of following the one who made us unique, different, and *in his image!*

In C. S. Lewis's *The Lion, the Witch and the Wardrobe*, the White Witch has turned many of the inhabitants of Narnia into stone, but Aslan, the Christ figure, jumps into the stone courtyard, pouncing on the statues, breathing life into them.

The courtyard looked no longer like a museum; it looked more like a zoo. Creatures were running after Aslan and dancing round him till he was almost hidden in the crowd. Instead of all that deadly white the courtyard was now a blaze of colors; glossy chestnut sides of centaurs, indigo horns of unicorns, dazzling plumage of birds, reddy-brown of foxes, dogs and satyrs, yellow stockings and crimson hoods of dwarfs; and the birch-girls in silver, and the beech-girls in fresh, transparent green, and the larch-girls in green so bright that it was almost yellow. And instead of the deadly silence the whole place rang with the sound of happy roarings, brayings, yelpings, barkings, squealings, cooings, neighings, stampings, shouts, hurrahs, songs and laughter.[2]

Lewis's summary of what is happening in Narnia is a brilliant description of what the church *should* look like: "The courtyard looked no longer like a museum; it looked more like a zoo." It is the incongruence and the oddness of our disjointed spirituality that ought to characterize every church. For God so loved the world, that whosoever believes in him will, from that point on, be considered weird by the rest of the world, which means the church should be more like a zoo than a tomb of identical mummies.

Unbalanced

Balance is a cherished value in modern society. Balance means that every negative is offset by an equal but opposite positive. Balance is a condition of neutrality in which the middle is considered desirable and healthy. When someone is described as balanced, it is understood as a compliment, implying that the person is well adjusted, sensible, and stable. Balanced describes a person who moderates all aspects of his or her life—physical, mental, social, and spiritual—and has found the perfect mix of all these attributes. Balance *sounds* like a characteristic of the Christian faith, like a goal to seek after or a quality worth cultivating. Balance *sounds* like a worthy ideal, a perfect description of a healthy follower of Christ.

Beware of balance.

Balance is a dangerous, illusionary characteristic and a temptress. Disguised as normal and sensible, it is silently destructive, crushing the unbalance of giftedness, taming the extremes of passion, smothering the raging fire of a genuine relationship with Jesus. Jesus was constantly criticized for being unbalanced. Think about it: Jesus could have healed six days a week and not upset anyone. People would have been just as healed on the second day of the week as they were on the Sabbath. Jesus could have sat down with the temple leaders and quietly discussed his theological reasoning for not allowing the place of worship to become a carnival of commerce. Instead, he crashed in like a crazy man with a whip and knocked over the tables, screaming and yelling and creating chaos. He certainly could have been more balanced.

In the book of Matthew, Jesus warns what happens when you decide to be his disciple.[3] His description of discipleship is virtually a *manual* of unbalance. Discipleship creates tension in families, can bring about financial ruin or destroy reputations. It sometimes makes enemies instead of friends, nomads instead of stable citizens. Jesus warned that the witness of our faith would create the perception that we are unbalanced, unstable, scary people to be around.

Think about how many of us have wondered why we don't fit, why our faith doesn't stabilize us, why we seem so out of sync with most of the world. Genuine faith is the isolating force in our lives that creates tension wherever we go. To put it another way, faith is the unbalancing force in our lives that is the fruit of God's disturbing presence.

One Sunday morning in our church, the pastor (that would be me) *and* the communion coordinator forgot that it was communion Sunday. During the middle of my sermon, the woman responsible for the communion table remembered. She looked at me and panicked, looked around the room, trying to think of what to do, then stood up, left the meeting room, and disappeared into the kitchen. A few minutes later, she reappeared with the wine and the bread, set up the table in front of me (I was still trying to preach), and sat down. I finished the sermon, finally, and moved into the communion service. I began with the words about the breaking of the bread: "On the night Jesus was betrayed, he took bread . . ." I reached down and uncovered the bread, and there in plain view was our communion loaf . . . *hot dog buns!*

The woman in charge of communion was not afraid to admit she had forgotten communion, she was not concerned about disrupting the service, and mostly, she did not want to put communion off another week. She *loves* communion, so she improvised from the meager stock in the kitchen. Her love for Christ drove her to risk being thought of as disruptive so we could celebrate what our church is *really* about—the body and blood of Jesus. Of course, she also gave us the most unusual communion service we've ever experienced and a memory none of us will ever forget, which is what happens when we allow people to express their uniqueness. Warm memories and godly surprises abound.

A number of years ago, a group of adults and high school students from our church traveled to Mexico to build houses. Most truck rental companies won't let you take their vehicles to Mexico because moving trucks are easily stolen. But the owner of the local truck rental company in our small town agreed to let us take a truck into Mexico. He trusted us—after all, we were building houses for Jesus. We filled our rented truck with clothes, building supplies, tents, food, and tools.

Once we crossed the border into Mexico, we headed for the federal toll highway between Tijuana and Ensenada. After paying the toll, we noticed a group of federal police parked on the side of the road. As we passed them, three tough-looking young policemen, each holding a large machine gun, waved us over. The three policemen walked up to our truck and asked me to step out of the cab. Standing in front of them, I could not believe how big and menacing those machine guns looked. The officer in the middle spoke in Spanish. One of our group members translated his short speech: "We are taking your truck. Please move out of the way." We pleaded with the police officer in the middle not to confiscate our truck, explaining that we were building houses for the poor and that we were doing this for Jesus. The more we talked, the more angry and demanding the officer became.

Suddenly one of the high school students, a sixteen-year-old foreign exchange student from Chile, interrupted the conversation. Politely but firmly, I took the young man aside and explained to him the seriousness of the situation. "Look," I said, "I know you want to help, but these soldiers are angry, and those machine guns look pretty convincing."

"Oh, I've seen lots of machine guns in our country," he replied confidently, unruffled by my warning. Before I could stop him, he grabbed the rental contract, walked over to the men, and began yelling at the officer in the middle, waving his hands and frantically pointing to the contract. Then he actually pushed his finger into the officer's chest.

I thought, *This is it; we're all headed for a Mexican jail.*

But the more the boy yelled, the more sheepish the federal guardsman looked, until, exasperated, he stopped the boy with a loud, "Vamos!"

Immediately the boy turned to me and said, "Get in the truck. Let's get out of here before he changes his mind." We jumped in and drove off in a cloud of dust.

As we fled the scene, I asked this young exchange student what he'd said to the guard that made him change his mind.

"I pointed to the contract and told him it said the truck was legal in Mexico and that he would be in a lot of trouble if we lost our truck," he replied happily.

"But the contract doesn't say that," I objected.

"I know, but the officer can't read English!" he told me.

Now, the young Chilean didn't act very spiritual—he lied![4] His spirituality certainly didn't look like spirituality. Our pursuit of spirituality is not always nice, nor is it sanitized. It often gets messy, landing more outside the lines than we think.

God Likes Odd People

It's difficult to be odd in a culture of sameness. Society is not kind to the odd, the strange, the different, the broken, and the outcast. But Jesus is. Sophisticated culture doesn't like aliens and rejects. But Jesus likes us. Most people would not choose odd people, but Jesus chooses us.

I wonder how many of us have turned away from Jesus, given up any hope of the spiritual life because we don't fit, because we aren't like everyone else, and because our Christianity seems so different and strange from the rest of the church's. I wonder if we realize how anxious Jesus is to reach out and walk with us arm and arm.

In his marvelous book *Letters to My Children*, Daniel Taylor describes an experience he had in the sixth grade. Periodically the students were taught how to dance. Thank God this kind of thing isn't done anymore, but the teacher would line up the boys at the door of the classroom to choose their partners. Imagine what it would have been like to be one of the girls waiting to be chosen, wondering if they were going to be chosen, wondering if they would be chosen by someone they didn't like.

One girl, Mary, was always chosen last. Because of a childhood illness, one of her arms was drawn up and she had a bad leg. She wasn't pretty, she wasn't smart, and she was . . . well . . . fat. The assistant teacher of Dan's class happened to attend his church. One day, she pulled Dan aside and said, "Dan, next time we have dancing, I want you to choose Mary." Dan couldn't believe it. Why would anyone pick Mary when there was Linda, Shelley, or even Doreen? Dan's teacher told him it is what Jesus would have done, and deep inside, he knew she was right, which didn't make it any easier. All Dan could hope for was that he would be last in line. That way, he could choose Mary, do the right thing, and no one would be the wiser. Instead, Dan was first in line.

The faces of the girls were turned toward me, some smiling. I looked at Mary and saw that she was only half-turned to the back of the room. (She knew no one would pick her first.) . . . Mr. Jenkins said, "Okay, Dan—choose your partner!"

I remember feeling very far away. I heard my voice say, "I choose Mary."

Never has reluctant virtue been so rewarded. I still see her face undimmed in my memory. She lifted her head, and on her face, reddened with pleasure and surprise and embarrassment all at once, was the most genuine look of delight and even pride that I have ever seen, before or since. It was so pure that I had to look away because I knew I didn't deserve it.

Mary came and took my arm, as we had been instructed, and she walked beside me, bad leg and all, just like a princess. . . .

Mary is my age now. I never saw her after that year. I don't know what her life's been like or what she's doing. But I'd like to think she has a fond memory of at least one day in sixth grade.

I know I do.[5]

There was nothing Mary could do. She was chosen, and she was chosen *first*. I have a feeling all of heaven stood and applauded not only Mary but all of the barking pigs out there who have decided to call themselves Christians. And when others say, "Christians don't act like you!" we respond, "Well, they do *now*."

6

unspiritual growth
Unprinciples of Erratic Discipleship

Dear God,
I think about you sometimes even when I'm not praying.
Elliott

CHILDREN'S LETTERS TO GOD

The church, by and large, has had a poor record of encouraging freedom. She has spent so much time inculcating in us the fear of making mistakes, that she has made us like ill-taught piano students: we play our songs, but we never really hear them because our main concern is not to make music but to avoid some flub that will get us in dutch.

ROBERT CAPON

Man has set out at tremendous speed . . . to go nowhere.

JACQUES ELLUL, THE PRESENCE OF THE KINGDOM

A woman described her dark night to me. "It's as if God lifted the lid of a music box in a dark room inside of me and then vanished. It's a beautiful turn, a new sound: and hearing it, I can't forget it. I'm like a child leaving my nursery, stumbling through a dark house in search of the Music Maker.

SUE MONK KIDD, *WHEN THE HEART WAITS*

I don't believe in spiritual growth.

Maybe I should clarify.

I don't believe in what most people *mean* by spiritual growth. Spiritual growth has become an industry, a system, a set of principles, formulas, training programs, curricula, books, and tapes which, if followed, promise to produce maturity and depth. Most of these programs are made up of the same ingredients: prayer, Bible study, service, and community. Duh. Authentic growth doesn't happen overnight. It can't be reduced to a formula (take some verses, wash down with a couple of prayers, and call me in the morning).

Yes, a regimen of prayer, Bible study, service, and community can and will contribute to spiritual growth, but that's like saying milk, vegetables, and chicken will contribute to my physical growth. Physical and spiritual growth cannot be reduced to mechanics. I'm all for getting the mechanics right, but spiritual growth is more than a procedure; it's a wild search for God in the tangled jungle of our souls, a search which involves a volatile mix of messy reality, wild freedom, frustrating stuckness, increasing slowness, and a healthy dose of gratitude.

Now are you ready to talk about spiritual growth? The kind of spiritual growth that begins with desire, not guilt; passion, not principles; desperation, not obligation? Are you ready to grow by traveling the road of failure, frustration, and surprise?

Let's get started.

In his book *The Easy Yoke,* Doug Webster tells a story about an idealistic college student who ended up on a mission trip to one of the more dangerous housing projects in Philadelphia. A brand-new Christian, this wide-eyed urban missionary didn't have a clue how to evangelize the inner city. Frightened and anxious to share his new faith, the young man approached a very large tenement house. Cautiously making his way through the dark, cluttered hallways, he gingerly climbed up one flight of stairs to an apartment. He knocked on the door, and a woman holding a naked, howling baby opened it. She was smoking and not in any mood to hear some white, idealistic college boy tell her about Jesus. She started cursing him and slammed the door in his face. The young man was devastated.

He walked out to the street, sat on the curb, and wept. *Look at me. How in the world could someone like me think I could tell anyone about Jesus?* Then he remembered that the baby was naked and the woman was smoking. The plan forming in his head didn't seem terribly *spiritual,* but . . .

He ran down the street to the local market and bought a box of diapers and a pack of cigarettes. When he knocked on the door again, he showed the woman his purchases. She hesitated and then invited him in. For the rest of the day, he played with the baby and changed its diapers (even though he had never changed diapers before). When the woman offered him a cigarette, even though he didn't smoke, he smoked. He spent the entire day smoking and changing diapers. Never said a word about Jesus. Late in the afternoon, the woman asked him why he was doing all this, and finally he got to tell her everything he knew about Jesus. Took about five minutes. When he stopped talking, the woman looked at him and said softly, "Pray for me and my baby that we can make it out of here alive," so he did.[1]

This college boy received a lesson in spiritual growth. In one frustrating afternoon, he learned about the power of sensitivity, the meaning of evangelism, the hopelessness of those who live in urban areas. He also learned that sometimes the Holy Spirit asks us to violate our convictions *for a season* in order to live the faith, not just talk about it. When this young man returned to college, he didn't start smoking, but he did start listening to the leading of the Holy Spirit. What an education! What a growth-producing experiment.

Can you imagine this young man standing in front of his congregation talking about his new program of smoking evangelism? It certainly would be an interesting evening. Doesn't sound much different than the day Jesus let a woman waste a bottle of expensive perfume on him. I have the feeling there was spiritual growth going on around the dinner table that night.

Messy Reality

One look at the book of Corinthians and it's clear the Christian life doesn't take place in the rarefied air of perfection. Paul wrote his letter to the church at Corinth to help them figure out what Christianity means in the everydayness of life. Paul gives us spectacular glimpses of Jesus while trying to deal with the messes which were occurring in the church: incestuous affairs, vicious lawsuits, divorce and separation, idol worship, overinflated egos, doctrinal infighting, jealousy, sexual promiscuity, and getting drunk during communion! And that was just one small congregation! Spiritual growth thrives in the midst of our problems, not in their absence. Spiritual growth occurs in the trenches of life, not in the classroom.

We don't grow while studying the definition of consistency; we grow when we try to *be* consistent in an inconsistent world. We can talk about love all we want, but loving those who are unlovely is how we learn about love. Jesus gave Peter some excellent teaching about betrayal and arrogance, but Peter didn't understand what Jesus was talking about *until he actually betrayed Jesus*. Peter's failure was the primary cause of his understanding and maturity.

So do we encourage people to fail so they can grow? No, we encourage people to grow, which means they will fail. We encourage each other to keep our eyes on Jesus, but we are not paranoid about failure. Paul himself said, "I'm not saying that I have this all together, that I have it made. But I am well on my way, reaching out for Christ, who has so wondrously reached out for me. Friends, don't get me wrong: By no means do I count myself an expert in all of this, but I've got my eye on the goal, where God is beckoning us onward—to Jesus. I'm off and running, and I'm not turning back."[2]

Wild Freedom

Freedom in Christ. What a nice concept. Sadly, most Christians are frightened of freedom. Ever since Jesus announced, "You shall know the truth and the truth will set you free," many in the church have tried to explain away his remark: "What Jesus meant is that we are free not to sin." Which is true. We are free not to sin. And we are also free to sin.

The radical truth of freedom in Christ is that I am free to choose good or bad, right or wrong, this way or that way. I can choose to run *to* Christ or run *away from* Christ. Freedom in Christ means I am free from everyone else's definition of freedom for *me*. Because I am free in Christ, when it comes to my relationship with him, he is the only one I answer to. Because

I am free in Christ, I am free from other people's concern that I might not use my freedom well. Paul said in 2 Corinthians 3:17, "And where the Spirit of the Lord is, there is freedom."

The psalmist said, "I will walk about in freedom, for I have sought out your precepts." Freedom clearly is connected to seeking out God's precepts, which means those who seek to follow God's commands are set free to roam in the wide open spaces of his love.

God's Word makes it clear he trusts us with freedom, even though it can be misused, even though he knows we might not be able to handle it. All he can do is leave us with his words, his precepts, and then let us figure out how a spiritual person would act in the context of our lives.

Frustrating Stuckness

I would like to add two words to our vocabulary of spiritual growth: *stuck* and *unstuck*. Most Christians consider being stuck a sign of failure or burnout, an indication that a person isn't working hard enough on their spiritual life. Being stuck means getting an F on our spiritual report card. The hidden assumption is, "If you are stuck in your spiritual life, you aren't doing something right, because dedicated Christians should *never* be stuck."

Nothing could be more untrue.

Actually, *getting stuck is the prerequisite to getting unstuck.*

Getting stuck is a great moment, a summons, a call from within, the glorious music of disaffection and dissatisfaction with our place in life. We get stuck when we want to change but can't, when we want to stop destructive behavior but don't, when the tug-o-war between God's will and ours stands still and we can't move. We're stuck going nowhere, unable to get beyond a particular point.

Getting stuck can be the best thing that could happen to us, because it forces us to stop. It halts the momentum of our lives. We have no choice but to notice what is around us, and we end up searching for Jesus. When we're stuck, we're much more likely to pay attention to our hunger for God and the longings and yearnings we have stifled. Sometimes being stuck is the low point and we say, "Okay, I give up." We cannot grow without first giving up and letting go. Getting stuck forces us to see the futility of our situation and to put life in perspective so that we can move on.

One summer day, our company staff was scheduled to participate in a ropes course. We had decided that we needed an experience that would bring our employees together and encourage us to work as a team. We had signed up to participate in both the low and the high courses.

Looming before us was the Centurion, a hundred-foot-high challenge. We each had to climb the tiniest of metal steps hammered into the side of a tree to reach the Plank, a small platform that narrowed to a six-foot length of two-by-twelve board. Standing on the end of the plank, you could look a hundred feet down into what appeared to be an abyss. About six feet away from the tip of the plank was a trapeze. The challenge was to leap from the plank and catch the trapeze with your hands like a circus performer.

My fear of heights has increased with age, and I had decided early in the day not to attempt the Centurion. One of the ropes-course staff kept stopping by to talk to me during the day, challenging me. "Come on, you can do the Centurion. I'll help you. I know you can do it." The sun was beginning to set and we had approximately fifteen minutes before we headed home. The young staff member persisted. "Let's go. I know you can do it. If you don't try, you'll regret it."

His persistence paid off; I decided to tackle the Centurion. I began my slow ascent. It seemed like hours before I reached the top, and when I did, everyone on the ground looked like ants. I was petrified. I sat on the plank, stuck. I could not move. But the longer I sat on the plank, the calmer I became, and my resolve started to build. After at least ten minutes of stuckness, I got to my feet, walked briskly to the end of the plank, hesitated a few seconds, and *jumped.*

I will never forget the exhilaration I felt as my hands grasped the trapeze and I swung back and forth. I was laughing uncontrollably, and I didn't want to let go. Finally, I let go and the belayer lowered me back to earth. I had been stuck all day, and even when I decided to climb the Centurion, I remained stuck on the plank, afraid to move. But my stuckness was preparing me for the jump. My mind was carrying on a dialogue with my fears, and after a lengthy discussion, my fears lost. I was ready to jump, and I did.

I don't know if words can explain what happened to me, but something inside changed. My fear of heights was lessened some, but more important, other obstacles in my life, decisions I had been avoiding, suddenly were less intimidating. My entire day of stuckness had resulted in a new confidence, a new courage to face the fears which had been plaguing me.

Faith creates its own kind of stuckness. Fear, unbelief, doubts. Years ago I heard an extraordinary story. I hope it's true. The pastor of a church in England announced to his congregation one Sunday that he was resigning because he no longer believed in Christianity. Stunned at first, the congregation gathered its composure, and the elders asked the pastor to meet with the congregation after the service. Everyone knew what was going to happen. His resignation would be accepted, financial arrangements would be made, and the search for a new pastor would begin.

But that's not what happened. The elders stood before the pastor and said, "Sir, we understand you have come to the painful conclusion that Christianity is not true. We believe it *is* true. In fact, we're so convinced it is true, we want you to stay on as our pastor. We want you to stand up each Sunday and preach your doubts to us. It's okay. We want to hear them, not so we can argue with you but so this can be a place where you can honestly seek the truth."

For three years, the pastor preached his doubts, and one morning he stood in the pulpit, looked out at the congregation with his eyes full of tears, and said, "I have found my faith again. Thank you for trusting the gospel; thank you for waiting for me to find my faith again!"

This pastor was stuck, burned out, lost, sinking in the quicksand of doubt, and his church *recognized his stuckness!* His congregation recognized that being stuck was a necessary stopping place where he could regroup, regain his strength, and move on. An extraordinary congregation of ordinary people understood their pastor's need to wrestle with the truth. Instead of talking about truth, they *trusted* the truth. They did not fear the waiting, nor did they fret over the "setbacks" they would have to endure when visitors came.

When the doubting pastor finally proclaimed his found-again faith, deep in his heart he must have whispered to God in gratitude, "Jesus has been hiding in these people all along."

Increasing Slowness

When my children were young, track meets filled part of each week during the spring. One particularly hot spring day, I attended a junior high track meet, arriving in the middle of the boys' 1500 meter race. During the last lap of the race, the audience stood, cheering two boys running side-by-side for the final fifty meters. A short distance behind them ran a pack of about four or five boys jockeying for third place. The crowd broke into applause for the first- and second-place finishers, and then crescendoed as the pack fought for third place.

Another runner suddenly caught my attention. As I looked down the track, I saw one boy lagging far behind. *Poor kid.* The portly seventh grader struggled for each breath, his face red and sweaty, the main artery in his neck bulging and throbbing to supply oxygen to his deprived muscles. Suddenly the woman to my left stepped over me and rushed down to the railing overlooking the track—obviously the boy's mother.

She screamed, "Johnny, *run faster!*"

I wish you could have seen the incredulous look on the boy's face. He had to be thinking, *Mom! I'm running as fast as I can!*

Spiritual growth does not happen by running faster.

What keeps many of us from growing is not sin but speed.

Most of us are just like Johnny. We are going as fast as we can, living life at a dizzying speed, and God is nowhere to be found. We're not rejecting God; we just don't have time for him. We've lost him in the blurred landscape as we rush to church. We don't struggle with the Bible, but with the clock. It's not that we're too decadent; we're too busy. We don't feel guilty because of sin, but because we have no time for our spouses, our children, or our God. It's not sinning too much that's killing our souls, it's our schedule that's annihilating us. Most of us don't come home at night staggering drunk. Instead, we come home staggering tired, worn out, exhausted, and drained because we live too fast.

Speed is not neutral. Fast living used to mean a life of debauchery; now it just means fast, *but the consequences are even more serious.* Speeding through life endangers our relationships *and* our souls.

Voices surround us, always telling us to move faster. It may be our boss, our pastor, our parents, our wives, our husbands, our politicians, or, sadly, even ourselves. So we comply. We increase the speed. We live life in the fast lane because we have no slow lanes anymore. *Every* lane is fast, and the only comfort our culture can offer is more lanes and increased speed limits. The result? Too many of us are running as fast as we can, and an alarming number of us are running much faster than we can sustain.

Speed damages our souls because living fast consumes every ounce of our energy. Speed has a deafening roar that drowns out the whispering voices of our souls and leaves Jesus as a diminishing speck in the rearview mirror.

Spiritual growth is not running faster, as in more meetings, more Bible studies, and more prayer meetings. Spiritual growth happens when we slow our activity down. If we want to meet Jesus, we can't do it on the run. If we want to stay on the road of faith, we have to hit the brakes, pull over to a rest area, and stop. Christianity is not about inviting Jesus to speed through life with us; it's about noticing Jesus sitting at the rest stop.

While the church earnestly warns Christians to watch for the devil, the devil is sitting in the congregation encouraging everyone to keep busy doing "good things." I just received a letter from a woman minister who was on the edge of crashing and burning. She and her family had joined a growing, active church and quickly volunteered to help. But two years later, she realized that her entire family was speeding by each other in unrestrained zeal to lead one activity or another at church every week.

"Run faster!" this woman's church bulletin screamed, but the only way she could save her soul from death was to slow down, which meant finding a new job.

Sin does not always drive us to drink; more often it drives us to exhaustion. Tiredness is equally as debilitating as drunkenness. *Burnout* is slang for an *inner* tiredness, a fatigue of our souls. Jesus came to forgive us all of our sins, including the sin of busyness. The problem with growth in the modern church is not the *slowness* of growth but the *rushing* of growth. Jesus came to give us rest.

We know we are ready for God to work in our lives when we're tired. When our lives begin to weigh us down, God is present in the heaviness. It turns out that it's weariness that's next to godliness, because when our souls are tired, we are able to hear his voice, and according to Matthew 11:28, what he's saying is, "Come. Rest."

The ugly truth, however, is that many of us *do not know how to rest!*

Actually, we do know how to rest; we simply refuse to rest. Rest is a decision we make. Rest is choosing to do nothing when we have too much to do, slowing down when we feel pressure to go faster, stopping instead of starting. Rest is listening to our weariness and responding to our tiredness, not to what is making us tired. Rest is what happens when we say one simple word: "No!" Rest is the ultimate humiliation because in order to rest, we must admit we are not necessary, that the world can get along without us, that God's work does not depend on us. Once we understand how unnecessary we are, only then might we find the right reasons to say yes. Only then might we find the right reasons to decide to *be* with Jesus instead of working for him. Only then might we have the courage to take a nap with Jesus.

Four Nonprinciples of Spiritual Growth

What kind of spirituality comes from the ingredients we've just discussed? The messy kind, the unpredictable, unique, ordinary-follower-of-Christ kind. But there's more. I want to give you some important "nonprinciples" of growth which are guaranteed to help you understand that there *are* no guarantees in the spiritual life, except for one: the longing for Jesus Christ is always underneath our every desire.

Nonprinciple 1: Spiritual Growth Encompasses a Lifetime of Decisions

We would all like to believe that growth results from one mighty decision, a once-and-for-all commitment to God. And while we should celebrate our initial decision to follow Christ, it's just the beginning of our spiritual journey, not the end. It is the first of many decisions, all of them important, all bringing growth.

Hundreds—maybe even thousands—of decisions make up genuine growth, some moving us closer to God, some moving us farther away, but all contributing to a deeper, richer, and more textured relationship with God.

During my adolescence, I made hundreds of decisions to become a Christian, to re-become a Christian, to rededicate my life to God, to rededicate my rededication, to go into full-time Christian service, to treat my parents better, to give God my hormones. I meant every one of those decisions, yet I successfully acted on most of them for only about two or three days. Still, those two or three days laid the groundwork for the next decision. I couldn't have made the next decision if I had not made the previous one. *I was growing one decision at a time.* No question about it, my growing looked inconsistent: two steps backward, one step forward, up and down, in and out, over and under. But I was growing all the same.

Nonprinciple 2: Spiritual Growth Looks Different for Each of Us

Growth cannot be charted as a steadily climbing line, *even though most people in the church believe spiritual growth should look like this:*

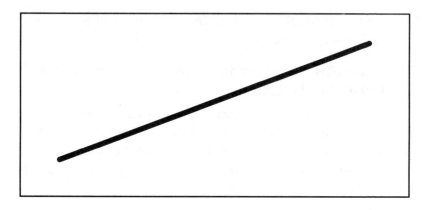

Spiritual growth—the frustrating and difficult attempt to find God's trail in the dusty terrain of our lives—can't be charted that easily. True spiritual growth looks different for each of us. If we were to graph real spiritual growth, it would look like this:

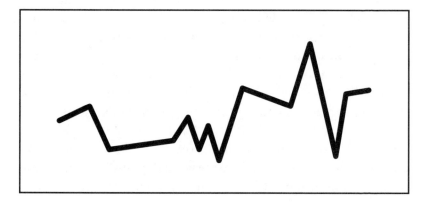

As you can see, it goes up, down, and sideways, giving it an irregular, jagged, odd shape. Genuine growth follows as many patterns as there are people. We uncover God's fingerprints in the dust of our busyness in a manner that's erratic, arbitrary, capricious, inconsistent, disjointed, and irregular. In spite of all the growth gurus and experts out there, we can't clone, manipulate, or systematize spiritual growth. We can't predict the unpredictable.

Usually when we analyze a graph like the first one, we make value judgments. The high spots represent the good or positive moments in our relationship with God, while the low spots represent the bad or negative moments. But what would happen if we removed value judgments from our thinking? What would happen if, in place of good and bad, positive and negative, high and low, we used words like resting, listening, waiting, starting, returning, savoring, celebrating, dancing, learning, growing? How would our understanding of the spiritual life be altered if we used these other words to describe our growing?

Maybe waiting is good and not waiting is bad. Maybe stopping has a higher value than starting. Maybe success is bad and failure is good. Suddenly the ups and downs of spiritual growth come into better focus. Some of us grow fast, some slow, some both fast and slow.

Nonprinciple 3: Give God 60 Percent

For years I believed it when people told me, "You either love God or you don't. You are either committed or you aren't. Give God 100 percent!" Sounds very spiritual, but the truth is there is no such thing as 100 percent commitment.

I am a morning person, so I wake up with a fairly high commitment level, say 73 percent. Then I go to work, and my commitment level drops to 45 percent. I get a raise, and my commitment level shoots up to 92 percent. My wife and I get in a fight, and it drops to 9 percent. And then *Baywatch* comes on television, and I'm up to 80 percent again (just kidding). Every day my commitment level moves up and down like a boat in rough seas, and my overall commitment might average out to 57 percent for the entire day. We *strive* for 100 percent, we *want* to give 100 percent (sometimes), we *wish* we could give 100 percent, but life isn't quite so simple.

Dr. Lorraine Monroe taught high school students in Harlem for many years. In her advanced English class one year sat a very bright student who, until this particular year, had shown great promise. This year his grades suddenly nose-dived, and he was obviously underperforming. Dr. Monroe met with the boy, challenged him, threatened him, pleaded with him, and counseled him. She tried everything, but he continued to float just above the fail line at about 70 percent. At the end of the school year, the young man barely passed, another casualty of the urban jungle.

Ten years later, Dr. Monroe was walking to work one morning when a well-dressed young man approached her.

"Do you remember me?" he asked.

"Of course I do," Dr. Monroe replied. "You were in my advanced English class many years ago. I remember you because you had so much talent and you wasted it in my class."

"I know, Dr. Monroe. I knew you believed in me, even though you were disappointed in my performance. I've always hoped I'd run into you again so I could thank you for believing in me, because I am one of the editorial writers for *Time* magazine now, and I owe much of my success to you. You see, Dr. Monroe, my senior year was a difficult year for my family. My father was in prison, my mother was a prostitute, my older brother was selling drugs in the projects, and I was left to care for my younger sister and brother. Dr. Monroe, 70 percent was 100 percent of all I could give you!"[3]

Sometimes a 70 percent commitment is 100 percent of all we have to give. And God is there, in the middle of our "meager" 70 percent, recognizing the seeds of growth in what we're giving him. God will show up in whatever percentage we give him, which motivates us to give even more.

Nonprinciple 4: Reluctant Growth Is Still Growth

No matter how much we've grown, we still need to grow more. No matter how mature we are, we never stop maturing. And no matter how unspiritual we are, as long as we want to grow more, Jesus will show up in the life of even the messiest of disciples. Take Daryl, for example.

Every month, the youth group at River Road Church visited Holcomb Manor, a local nursing home, to hold church services for the residents. Daryl, a reluctant youth group volunteer, did not like nursing homes. For a long time, he had avoided the monthly services. But when a flu epidemic depleted the group of sponsors, Daryl agreed to help with the next month's service, as long as he did not have to be part of the program.

During the service, Daryl felt awkward and out of place. He leaned against the back wall, between two residents in wheelchairs. Just as the service finished and Daryl was thinking about a quick exit, someone grabbed his hand. Startled, he looked down and saw a very old, frail, and obviously lonely man in a wheelchair. What could Daryl do but hold the man's hand? The man's mouth hung open, and his face held no expression. Daryl doubted whether he could hear or see anything.

As everyone began to leave, Daryl realized he didn't want to leave the old man. Daryl had been left too many times in his own life. Caught somewhat off-guard by his feelings, Daryl leaned over and whispered, "I'm . . . uh . . . sorry, I have to leave, but I'll be back. I promise." Without warning, the man squeezed Daryl's hand and then let go. As Daryl's eyes filled with tears, he grabbed his stuff and started to leave.

Inexplicably, he heard himself say to the old man, "I love you," and he thought, *Where did that come from? What's the matter with me?*

Daryl returned the next month and the month after that. Each time, it was the same. Daryl would stand in the back, Oliver would grab his hand, Daryl would say he had to leave, Oliver would squeeze his hand, and Daryl would say softly, "I love you, Mr. Leak." (He had learned his name, of course.) As the months went on, about a week before the Holcomb Manor service, Daryl would find himself looking forward to visiting his aged friend.

On Daryl's sixth visit, the service started, but Oliver still hadn't been wheeled out. Daryl didn't feel too concerned at first, because it often took the nurses a long time to wheel everyone out. But halfway into the service, Daryl became alarmed. He went to the head nurse. "Um, I don't see Mr. Leak here today. Is he okay?" The nurse asked Daryl to follow her and led him to room 27.

Oliver lay in his bed, his eyes closed, his breathing uneven. At forty years of age, Daryl had never seen someone dying, but he knew that Oliver was near death. Slowly, he walked to the side of the bed and grabbed Oliver's hand. When Oliver didn't respond, tears filled Daryl's eyes. He knew he might never see Oliver alive again. He had so much he wanted to say, but the words wouldn't come out. He stayed with Oliver for about an hour, then the youth director gently interrupted to say they were leaving.

Daryl stood and squeezed Mr. Leak's hand for the last time. "I'm sorry, Oliver, I have to go. I love you." As he unclasped his hand, he felt a squeeze. Mr. Leak had responded! He had squeezed Daryl's hand! The tears were unstoppable now, and Daryl stumbled toward the door, trying to regain his composure.

A young woman was standing at the door, and Daryl almost bumped into her. "I'm sorry," he said, "I didn't see you."

"It's all right, I've been waiting to see you," she said. "I'm Oliver's granddaughter. He's dying, you know."

"Yes, I know."

"I wanted to meet you," she said. "When the doctors said he was dying, I came immediately. We have always been very close. They said he couldn't talk, but he's been talking to me. Not much, but I know what he is saying. Last night he woke up. His eyes were bright and alert. He looked straight into my eyes and said, 'Please say goodbye to Jesus for me,' and he laid back down and closed his eyes.

"He caught me off guard, and as soon as I gathered my composure, I whispered to him, 'Grandpa, I don't need to say goodbye to Jesus; you're going to be with him soon, and you can tell him hello.'

"Grandpa struggled to open his eyes again. This time his face lit up with a mischievous smile, and he said as clearly as I'm talking to you, 'I know, but Jesus comes to see me every month, and he might not know I've gone.' He closed his eyes and hasn't spoken since.

"I told the nurse what he'd said, and she told me about you, coming every month, holding Grandpa's hand. I wanted to thank you for him, for me . . . and, well, I never thought of Jesus as being as chubby and bald as you, but I imagine that Jesus is very glad to have had you be mistaken for him. I know Grandpa is. Thank you."

She leaned over and kissed Daryl on the forehead.

Oliver Leak died peacefully the next morning.[4]

If a reluctant follower like Daryl can be mistaken for Jesus, maybe you and I can too.

7

little graces
The Triumph of Tiny Living

Something is better than nothing.

UNKNOWN

Just one person running loose in Southern California who can say "no" can cause a revival. You don't have to be that good of a Christian to make other Christians. You can just be a little Christian running around saying, "No, we don't do that."

WILL WILLIMON, *WITTENBURG DOOR*

One of the most insidious maladies of our time [is]: the tendency in most of us to observe rather than act, avoid rather than participate, not do rather than do; the tendency to give in to the sly, negative, cautionary voices that constantly counsel us to be careful, to be controlled, to be wary and prudent and hesitant and guarded in our approach of this complicated thing called living.

ARTHUR GORDON, *A TOUCH OF WONDER*

During the last months of World War II, the British conducted daily bombing raids over Berlin. The bombers would take off from an airstrip in England and fly surrounded by smaller fighter planes whose job it was to keep German fighters from attacking the bombers, which were easy targets.

One night after a successful bombing raid, as they were heading for the safety of England, the bombers were attacked by a large group of German fighter planes. Somehow, during the dogfight, one bomber found itself flying alone with no protection, and suddenly, a German fighter appeared out of nowhere. The crew of the bomber watched as the German plane moved closer and closer, until finally, it was in range. They prepared for the worst and watched helplessly as tracer bullets began spitting from the fighter. Bullets whizzed by them, over and under, until *Thud! Thud! Thud! Thud! Thud!* Five bullets slammed into the fuselage of the bomber near the gas tank. The crew braced for the explosion, but nothing happened. They could see fuel pouring from the bullet holes, but there was no explosion. Miraculously, they were able to make it back to their base and get safely off the plane.

A few hours after they had landed, one of the mechanics showed up in the crew's barracks. He had found five bullets inside the fuel tanks, crumpled but not exploded. He handed them to the pilot. The pilot carefully opened the shells and to the crew's amazement found each one empty of gunpowder. Inside one was a tiny wad of paper. When he unfolded the paper, he found a note which read, "We are Polish POWs— forced to make bullets in factory. When guards do not look, we do not fill with powder. Is not much, but is best we can do. Please tell family we are alive."

The note was signed by four Polish prisoners of war.[1]

Five tiny bullets, out of millions and millions of bullets made during the war, made all the difference for the crewmen of a British bomber.

The power of goodness is found in the tiny. Since the beginning, God has chosen the tiny over the large: David over Goliath, Gideon and his three hundred soldiers over thousands of Midianites, Elijah over the prophets of Baal, one sheep over the ninety-nine sheep. Spirituality is about doing the tiny work of God, little acts, small responses to God's presence in our lives. Every week, my church shows me heroic acts by ordinary people who never will be recognized.

Because we have heard the biblical stories over and over again, we have exaggerated the size of the tiny ministry Jesus actually had. Yes, there were the crowds, but even when there were crowds, he tried to avoid them, escape them, run from them. Jesus was around for three years, and he really didn't do all that much. He hung out with a few guys, healed a leper or two and a couple of lame folk and a blind guy, made some wine, helped out three or four women, raised one person from the dead, calmed down a crazy person or two, caused a scene in the temple, and then disappeared.

Think what Jesus could have accomplished if he'd stayed on earth for twenty, thirty, or fifty more years. Wow, think what he could have done with all the technology available today!

Nope. Jesus showed up for a little while, did a few tiny miracles, said a few amazing words, and left.

But his few tiny acts changed the world forever. Tiny becomes huge when Jesus is involved.

It is easy for us to get the impression that God is about big, spectacular, and miraculous. After reading a few books, watching television, and listening to the stories at church, it is very easy to conclude that unless God is doing really big things through our lives, we're not spiritual.

Spiritual people are about tiny things, which is the fruit of their spirituality. The spiritual life is not a life of success; it is a life of faithfulness, and it's not easy. God does "big" things once in a while, but there is no question that the primary work of God in the world is salt-and-light tiny. God knew we would naturally be dazzled by big; that's why Jesus told the parables of the lost sheep, the lost coin, the lost son, the mustard seed. Jesus was trying to tell us something: the spiritual life is a tiny life, filled with little decisions, tiny steps toward God, tiny glimpses of his presence, little changes and small movings, tiny successes and imperceptible stirrings.

Stuck in the book of Mark is a four-verse story which is more like an aside than a significant event.[2] Jesus has just been ranting about excessive displays of arrogance and showy spirituality. As he finishes his rather heated criticism of those who want everyone to notice their piety, he sees a woman whom no one notices. Jesus recognizes the unmistakable look of poverty: clothes tattered, one ragged piece of clothing piled over the other (she was cold, the elderly are always cold), stained with years of dirt. Shuffling across the temple grounds, she drops two thin coins in the temple collection box. Talk about an unimpressive moment! Old woman gives little gift. Nice story, but not the stuff movies are made of. As much as we would like to be moved by this woman's sacrifice, it doesn't come close to the life-threatening drama of the disciples and heroes of the faith.

Which is what makes the story of the widow powerful. It isn't dramatic, spectacular, revolutionary, significant, or amazing. Here is a woman whom no one notices and, worse, whom no one *cares* to notice. In the world she lives in, she is part of the landscape, a blur in a crowd of faces, but she is a *faithful blur,* an inconspicuous lover of God who *loves* God every day and *lives* God every day. *She doesn't care whether she is noticed;* she cares about whether God is noticed. Whether she understands it or not, Jesus understands the power of people who couldn't care less about being noticed. Christianity shows itself most powerfully in the unnoticed life, in the inconspicuous servant, the unrecognized saint, the invisible disciple.

We shouldn't be surprised. Jesus chose not to change the world with armies, swords, legions of angels, and lightning bolts. Instead, he changed the world by rejecting fame and welcoming the infamy of a criminal's death.

Tiny living is critical to our times because the media has an insatiable hunger for big. The firemen and police who died in the World Trade Center collapse on September 11 were genuine heroes, and we are all glad for them, but they were big heroes in a big story. The reality is, there are also millions of tiny heroes. Heroes who never make it on television or in the newspapers but are heroes nonetheless. The stories I am about to tell are not meant to glamorize or make heroes out of people; they are meant to encourage all of us to recognize the power of the ordinary, the significance of the insignificant, the eternal difference ordinary, messy, unfinished, under-construction people like you and me can make. Let me give you examples of tiny actions by a few inconspicuous, unnoticed disciples who have bought into the foolish, upside-down, invisible kingdom of God.

Michael: the Boy Who Unchained His Mother from Depression

Michael's physical and mental disabilities required him to live in a twenty-four-hour care facility. Michael could walk but needed assistance with almost everything else, and his speech was impaired, making his words difficult to understand. His parents lived some distance away, and periodically, Michael's mother suffered from bouts of depression brought on by guilt for not being able to care for her son. During one depressive episode, she stayed in bed for days, unresponsive to all efforts to engage her, even her husband's. Concerned, Michael's father asked him to come home to see if his presence could bring her out of her deep despair.

When he arrived home, Michael went straight into his mother's bedroom and sat on her bed. He stayed with her for a long time but said nothing. When his father walked into the bedroom, Michael pointed to a large flower vase and repeated over and over again, "Ca ... ca ... ca ... oke." It took his father a while to understand that Michael was asking him to fill the vase with Coke.

After the father filled the vase, Michael slowly and painfully walked into the kitchen, returning with a small piece of bread. Tenderly, he took hold of his mother's hand and placed the bread in it. He then dipped the bread into the Coke and gently lifted the bread to his mother's mouth as he began stumbling through the words of the communion service. His mother's eyes filled with tears as she took the bread, and within a few hours, she came out of her depression. Michael did what he could, his mother's descent into depression stopped, and her recovery began.

Michael might not have been able to do many things, but he could *feel!* His speech might have been impaired, but his heart worked fine. His impromptu communion service might seem unbalanced to some, but it's what helped his mother regain *her* balance. Michael had one gift even his father didn't have: *he knew what his mother needed.* Michael trusted what he could do instead of getting frustrated about what he couldn't do, and then he committed a tiny act of discipleship.

Michael could have lamented his limitations; he could have despaired about the impossibility of bringing his mother out of depression; he could have suggested his father hire a "professional" to help his mother. Instead, he did what Christians do when they don't know what to do. He went to the arsenal of weapons which separate the church from every other organization and decided on one of the most unlikely: communion. Michael realized the foolishness of God is still more powerful than all the brilliant weapons of our culture.

Lisa: the Girl Who Made Winners out of Losers

Lisa (not her real name) decided to try out for the high school track team. Her rural school had so few students that anyone who tried out for a sport made the team. Aspiration rather than ability determined who would make the roster.

Through mere desire, Lisa became the anchor runner on the girls' 1500 meter relay team. Because her school boasted the only girls' 1500 relay team in its small league, Lisa and her running mates received an invitation to represent their league in the section finals. Everyone knew the team had no chance to beat the more talented, experienced teams, yet before the race, Lisa continually flashed a brilliant smile as if she were relaxed and enjoying herself.

Puzzled, a friend of mine asked Lisa why she was so calm. "I love the relay!" she said. "We're not very fast. I'm always the last one to finish, so when I come down the stretch, the people in the stands cheer for me."

Sure enough, by the final lap, Lisa's team lagged far behind. As Lisa rounded the last turn, running hard for the finish line, everyone else had already left the track, but her smile lit up the course. The crowd came to its feet, cheering as Lisa crossed the finish line.

"See," Lisa later told my friend, "we always get a standing ovation, and we're last. I love it."

Lisa's my hero.

She has rejected the values of a culture that worships winning. She refuses to listen to those who say, "Second is just the first to lose." Lisa has decided that last can be as good as first. In her unknown corner of the world, she triumphs over those who would call her a loser.

I am reminded of a small group of "losers" who stood by the cross while Jesus died. Just a few days earlier, thousands had cheered Jesus. Next thing you know, he's dying and alone, and a few of his friends decide they will stick with him as he dies. I am also reminded of a list of "unimpressive unknowns" in Romans chapter 16 (except that they *were* impressive). Listen to Paul's description of their heroic smallness:

- Phoebe: a servant of the church
- Priscilla and Aquila: a church meets in their house
- Mary, Tryphena, Tryphosa, and Persis: women who worked hard
- Andronicus and Junias: have been in prison with me

Godly people, "tested and approved in Christ," doing the tiny things Paul depended on for his survival. The church was growing, spreading, adding thousands to its rolls every day, and yet Paul takes time to affirm and thank the people who had not forgotten him.

Claudio and Virgilio: the Boys Who Remembered One Unremembered

One third of Brazil's 150 million residents are under fourteen years of age. Twenty-five million children live in desperate poverty. Eight million are abandoned, needy, and walk the streets. Thirty-five percent of these boys and girls die on the streets before they reach the age of eighteen.

A group of us had come to São Paulo to see firsthand the tragedy of the street kids of Brazil. We met Virgilio and Claudio, street kids themselves at one time, now giving their lives to reach the unreachable. As we walked toward a freeway underpass where many of the street children live (if you can call it living), we found ourselves stranded on a cement divider between four lanes of heavily traveled highway. Traffic sped by in both directions, making it impossible to cross the street.

Suddenly, in front of us, we saw an emaciated young boy sleeping on the cement divider, using his hands as a pillow. How could someone sleep so soundly despite the noise and confusion of thousands of cars, the smothering heat, and the unending commotion of the city? I asked Claudio. He told me the boy was sleeping off a crack high.

"Sometimes they can sleep for twenty-four hours, and you don't want to wake them," Claudio warned, "because the crack can make them very dangerous."

I passed by the boy, but when I turned back, I saw Claudio bending down slowly, gently, touching the boy and speaking very softly, "Andrew. Andrew." He spoke with amazing compassion and care. The boy did not wake up, and we kept walking.

Later Claudio told me the boy's story. Fourteen years old, Andrew was a crack addict who had once been involved in Claudio's rehabilitation project, but the lure of the street proved too much.

That night as I sat in my room, thinking about Andrew and Claudio and Virgilio, I could not stop the tears. Reaching eight million street kids is an overwhelming responsibility. Most of the eight million are like forgotten grains of sand. What's the point?

Claudio and Virgilio see it differently. Because of their ministry, only 7,999,999 grains are left, and one grain, Andrew, is not forgotten. Thank God for those who remember the forgotten! Thank God for two unknown men who have given their lives to saving one tiny grain of sand at a time.

Sue: the Woman Whose Silence Silenced the Angry

A group of us were at a spiritual retreat when an innocent late-night discussion escalated into a toxic disagreement that exploded into an extremely angry argument. Provoked and frustrated, we all went to bed upset. The next morning, we requested help from one of our spiritual directors, Sue, who graciously agreed to mediate the situation. Early in the afternoon, we gathered in a small room and started unraveling the argument of the night before. As the discussion went on, the tension in the room escalated as ugly words shot back and forth. Anger again filled the room. Meanwhile, our spiritual director remained silent, making no attempt to mediate whatsoever. *What was the matter with her? Why wasn't she intervening?* Our discomfort increased until our director's silence became so loud we stopped arguing. One by one, we looked up to see Sue quietly sobbing, her eyes reddened, her face distorted with anguish at our pain.

Without saying a word, our spiritual director broke through the anger in the room, silenced our shouting, connected with the deep cause of our bickering, and put us on the road to reconciliation. Even though Sue did not understand the complicated, dysfunctional relationships among the members of our group, God used her silence and her tears to begin a process of healing.

Gertie: the Old Lady Who Infiltrated a Youth Group

At seventy-six years of age, Gertie became concerned about the young people in her church, so she volunteered to help with the high school youth group.

"What would you like to do?" the pastor asked.

"I don't know," she said. "God and I will think of something."

Gertie wasn't a speaker, she felt too old to play games, and she didn't want to lead Bible studies or counsel at camp. But she had a camera, so she took pictures of every kid in the youth group, put them on flash cards, and wrote biographical information on the back of each. She memorized the picture and the information on each flash card, then stood at the door to the youth room every Sunday night. As the students entered, she welcomed each one by name. At the end of the meeting, Gertie stood at the door again, saying goodbye to each person by name and promising to pray. Over the years, the church's young people discovered that Gertie had the Bible almost memorized, so they came to her with the questions and struggles of their young lives.

Ten years of youth ministry later, at eighty-six, Gertie suffered three strokes. The prospect of her death distressed all the kids in the youth group. They wanted to help her, to tell her how much she meant to them, but they didn't know how. One afternoon after he'd finished reading *Tuesdays with Morrie,* the youth leader had an idea.

"Gertie," he told her, "I want to do your funeral."

"I know," she said, "I *want* you to do my funeral . . . but I'm not dead yet."

"Yes, but I want to do your funeral while you are *alive,* so that you can hear just how much you mean to our youth group and our church."

Gertie loved the idea, and the youth group and its leader planned her living funeral.

As you might imagine, young men and women packed out the service. Many of them had graduated from college, married, and had children of their own. Ten years' worth of students shared Gertie stories that night.

At the end of the evening, a group of high school young people gathered mysteriously at the back of the room. To understand what they were doing, you need to know something about Gertie. She may have been eighty-six, but she never lost her youth. No old people's perfume for Gertie; she loved expensive designer perfumes like Estée Lauder's Beautiful, which was her favorite.

The young people walked down the aisle, all clumped together in order to hide something. When they arrived up front, they held up a giant, expensive bottle of Beautiful, which they broke and poured over Gertie's feet, anointing her in gratitude for all she had done. Like the widow, Gertie had given what she could. And like the widow with her tiny offering, Gertie's offering will live on long after she's gone.[3]

Michael, Lisa, Claudio, Virgilio, Sue, and Gertie might not show up on the radar screens of the movers and shakers of the world. But God recognizes them, and he recognizes the other unrecognizables like you and me. Every tiny contribution we make to his kingdom is noticed and remembered, and one day we will understand just how beautiful our thin sacrifices are.

Tiny Mosaic

Morehead, Minnesota, the home of Concordia College, lies across the state line from Fargo, North Dakota, a very bleak part of the country (especially during the winter). All year, the community anticipates Concordia's annual Christmas concert. Each December, a huge choir and a full orchestra give a musical performance in the concert hall at the college.

Every year, the people in the community create a unique background for the concert—a one-hundred-by-thirty-foot mosaic. Beginning in the summer, about six months before the concert, the community designs a new mosaic, rents an empty building, and the painting begins. Thousands of people, from junior high schoolers to senior citizens, paint the mosaic. They paint by number on a large-scale design that has thousands and thousands of tiny pieces. Day after day, month after month, one little painted piece at a time, the picture on the mosaic gradually takes shape.

When everyone has finished painting, an artist goes over the entire creation, perfecting the final work of art. When the mosaic is completed, they place it behind the choir. It has the appearance of an enormous, beautiful stained-glass window. The weekend of the concert, those people who helped paint arrive early, along with their friends and neighbors. Throughout the building, you can hear people whispering, "See that little green spot below the camel's foot? I painted it."

Every year in the middle of the summer in Morehead, Minnesota, thousands of unknown, ordinary people paint a tiny insignificant tile. Six months later, the result is a spectacularly beautiful masterpiece.

Our tiny choices and tiny moves toward God may not seem like much. But someday you and I will stand together in the great cathedral of heaven, and up front, by Jesus, will hang the most magnificent mosaic we could ever imagine, made up of thousands and thousands of our tiny responses to God's love in our lives.

8

God's annoying love

The Irresistibleness of Grace

All the persons of faith I know are sinners, doubters, uneven performers. We are secure not because we are sure of ourselves but because we trust that God is sure of us.

EUGENE PETERSON, *A LONG OBEDIENCE IN THE SAME DIRECTION*

"Does God like you?" I asked a five-year-old little girl. She stifled a grin. She is a compassionate soul. "Yep," she said easily, confidently, certainly. "How do you know?" "Because of the way he talks to me. He just likes me. I recognize it in his voice."

ROBERT BENSEN, *BETWEEN THE DREAMING AND THE COMING TRUE*

I will not leave you alone. You are mine. I know each of My sheep by name. You belong to Me. If you think I am finished with you, if you think I am a small god

> *that you can keep at a safe distance, I will pounce*
> *upon you like a roaring lion, tear you to pieces, rip*
> *you to shreds, and break every bone in your body.*
> *Then I will mend you, cradle you in my arms, and*
> *kill you tenderly.*
>
> BRENNAN MANNING, *LION AND LAMB*

I had a paper route when I was eleven years old. It was one of the more difficult routes, sprinkled with farms, rural homes, and a smattering of hills. But the money was good for a child, and my parents allowed me to keep my earnings to buy the non-necessities of life (stereo, records, tape recorders, etc.). Our family's lower-middle-class income had very little room for non-necessities. My monthly income forced me to learn about delayed gratification, savings accounts, and other nuances of capitalism.

One ordinary Tuesday, while cruising downtown on my bicycle, I passed by a music store and skidded to a halt. There, in the window, standing all by itself, was the most beautiful conga drum I had ever seen. It was almost as tall as me, and I could not take my eyes off its barrel-shaped beauty. Dark and light wood alternated around a laminated exterior. A round, chrome frame stretched the thick animal skin tightly over the top of the drum. It was 1953, and an eleven-year-old boy could not resist the allure of such a drum. Twenty dollars was a lot of money in those days, *but I had twenty dollars in my savings account.* Before the day was over, I had purchased the conga drum, brought it home, and proudly showed it to all my friends. None of us knew how to play any kind of a drum, but it didn't stop us from pretending to be the most rhythmically talented group of boys in the world.

And then my father arrived home from work. Anxious to show him my new purchase, I pranced into the kitchen beating on my drum as loudly as I could, beaming from ear to ear.

"Where did you get that?" my dad said sharply.

I hesitated. "Uh, I bought it with my paper route money, Dad. It's a conga drum! Isn't it beautiful?" I was very proud.

His harshness continued. "How much did you pay for it?"

"Twenty dollars," I said meekly, still waiting for him to share my excitement and joy.

"Twenty dollars?" I was not prepared for his anger. I stood there stupidly while my new drum slowly slid from my side onto the kitchen floor. Nothing but silence, and then the words I shall never forget: "Take it back!"

I couldn't believe what I was hearing. My parents had emphasized over and over again that my paper route money was mine. As long as I didn't spend it on something illegal or immoral, I was free to buy what I wanted. I wanted the conga drum, and my father was ordering me to take it back. (My father had grown up during the Great Depression. In fairness to him, he thought the music store salesman had taken advantage of me. Of course, I didn't understand that at the time.)

The next morning, I took the drum back. For reasons I don't really understand, the trauma of that experience burned itself deep into my soul. Emotionally, I was crushed, and every good experience since has been shadowed by the fear of hearing the words "Take it back." Buried in the back of my mind is the gnawing worry that my grace credit card is going to be cancelled. Parked somewhere in my subconscious is the belief that grace and forgiveness are lavish, unconditional, and *limited.*

Cross Jesus one too many times, fail too often, sin too much, and God will decide to take his love back. It is so bizarre, because I know Christ loves me, but I'm not sure he likes me, and I continually worry that God's love will simply wear out. Periodically, I have to be slapped in the face with Paul's words in Romans: "I am convinced that neither death nor life, neither angels nor demons, neither the present nor the future, nor any powers, neither height nor depth, nor anything else in all creation, *will be able to separate us from the love of God that is in Christ Jesus our Lord.*"[1]

God's Love Is Sticky

Paul uses lots of religious words here, but the bottom line is we are all stuck with God's love whether we want to be or not. The words "nor anything else in all creation" mean that *nothing* can stop God from loving us. Nothing. He just keeps loving us. In modern language, you could say, "Neither failure nor poor church attendance, nor inadequate Bible reading and prayer, nor betrayal, denial, doubt, insecurity, guilt, weakness, bad theology, or even losing our temper can separate us from the love of God." He loves us when we don't want him to love us. He loves us when we don't act like Christians. He loves us when our lives are a mess. His love is sticky, resistant to rejection, aggressive, and persistent. The challenge is on, so go ahead—resist his love, run from it, hide from it. Go ahead and try.

In the movie *The Great Santini,* Bull Meechum is a marine who cannot leave his military training at the office. His children (he calls them "hogs," just like new recruits) are awakened early every morning and ordered to stand in line for "inspection." As blustery and difficult as he is, Bull's four children love and respect their father. Children can tell when they are loved, and although Daddy has a tough exterior, they know he loves them. But Daddy, like every daddy, has his share of flaws.

All his life, Bull has been fighting the demons of his childhood with a father who was never satisfied, always demanding more from his son. Bull and his oldest son, Ben, have a very close relationship, which begins to fall apart as the son matures.

Late one evening, Bull staggers into his house drunk and begins to physically abuse his wife. Hearing their mother's screams, the children jump out of their beds, race down the stairs, and attempt to restrain their father. Ben grabs Bull by the collar and throws him against the wall while the other three children try to grab his legs and arms. When the screaming and crying die down, Bull stumbles backward and drunkenly realizes he has come to the edge of destroying his marriage and his family. Humiliated, angry, and mostly incoherent, he backs away from his family and storms outside.

Later, after the children are quieted down and in bed, Ben finds his mother standing on the porch. "I'm getting worried," she says. "Your father may be in trouble."

"Good," Ben snaps, "I hope he dies."

"No you don't," his mother protests. "I want you to go get him."

Ben reluctantly searches for his father in the empty streets near their house. At last, he finds Bull slumped against a tree mumbling a sad imaginary dialogue with his father. As the son listens to his father's tearful words, he begins to understand why his dad is the way he is. Finally, Bull lays down on the grass, crying, and his son stoops to pick him up. "Come on, Dad, let's go home. I think I understand now."

As he picks up his father, he gently says, "I love you, Dad." Bull pushes him away and staggers across the park. Ben, angry at first, keeps saying, "I love you, Dad. I love you." Bull tries to escape his son, but Ben starts circling him, taunting him, "I love you, Dad. Come on, Dad, I love you! Stop me, Dad, come on, stop me! I love you, Dad."

Finally, when it becomes clear to Bull that he cannot escape or run away from his son's love, Ben picks him up and helps him home.

Bull is angered by his son's unconditional, relentless, stubborn love. No matter how ugly he becomes, his son refuses to stop loving him. He doesn't deserve Ben's love, and he knows it. He has been a flawed, bullheaded father. He has failed many times—too many. He tries to drown out Ben's words, but he can't.

Ben reminds us of a God who refuses to stop loving us no matter the mess we've made of our lives. He refuses to exclude us. That is why he finally had to send us Jesus.

Until Jesus came along, we were all outside the fence of God's grace.

In the Second World War, a group of soldiers was fighting in the rural countryside of France. During an intense battle, one of the American soldiers was killed. His comrades did not want to leave his body on the battlefield and decided to give him a Christian burial. They remembered a church a few miles behind the front lines whose grounds included a small cemetery surrounded by a white fence. After receiving permission to take their friend's body to the cemetery, they set out for the church, arriving just before sunset.

A priest, his bent-over back and frail body betraying his many years, responded to their knocking. His face, deeply wrinkled and tan, was the home of two fierce eyes that flashed with wisdom and passion.

"Our friend was killed in battle," they blurted out, "and we wanted to give him a church burial."

Apparently the priest understood what they were asking, although he spoke in very broken English. "I'm sorry," he said, "but we can bury only those of the same faith here."

Weary after many months of war, the soldiers simply turned to walk away. "But," the old priest called after them, "you can bury him outside the fence."

Cynical and exhausted, the soldiers dug a grave and buried their friend just outside the white fence. They finished after nightfall.

The next morning, the entire unit was ordered to move on, and the group raced back to the little church for one final goodbye to their friend. When they arrived, they couldn't find the gravesite. Tired and confused, they knocked on the door of the church. They asked the old priest if he knew where they had buried their friend. "It was dark last night and we were exhausted. We must have been disoriented."

A smile flashed across the old priest's face. "After you left last night, I could not sleep, so I went outside early this morning and *I moved the fence*."[2]

Jesus did more than move the fence; he tore it down. No wonder he made the scribes and Pharisees nervous; fence *makers* do not like their fences torn down.

God's Grace Is Unfair

Jesus told a parable which by anyone's standards is offensive, discriminatory, elitist, ridiculous, and very annoying.[3] Early in the morning, a wealthy landowner hires some unemployed men to work his vineyard at an agreed upon price (one denarius). As the day progresses, he hires more workers, promising to pay them fairly. He hires workers at nine, noon, three, and as late as five in the afternoon. At the end of the day, the foreman, following the landowner's instructions, pays the workers in order, starting with the last ones who were hired. The latecomers who worked only an hour or so received one denarius. Those who worked longer reasoned that they would, of course, receive more. But they didn't. Everyone received one denarius *no matter how long they had worked.* Today, the landowner would be sued, and he would lose. Given the level of rage in today's world, the workers probably would have assaulted him or damaged his property. Who could blame them? Who of us would not have sympathy for a person who worked eight hours and received only as much as a person who worked one hour? It's not fair.

Let's be honest, this landowner would be out of touch in the modern world, or with any democratic society, for that matter. Civilized people do not behave this way. We believe in equality, fairness, and the right to be paid equitably. We have laws to protect us from arbitrary, capricious, unfair employers. What is even more disturbing is Jesus' explanation of the parable. He says that *the kingdom of God is like this!* What? Wait a minute. If there is one eternal constant, one attribute of God we can trust unequivocally, it is God's fairness. God is the eternal monitor of fairness, isn't he? Life may not be fair, but God is definitely fair, right?

Not according to this parable. Generous? Yes. Fair? No. We should have known. Jesus gives us plenty of warning. The last will be first. You have to die to live. Clearly Jesus' love is more than radical; it is arbitrary, bewildering, shocking, and offensive. None of us wants to admit it, but if *we* had started work at sunrise, we would have resented those who had worked only an hour and received the same pay. Loving everyone is a great concept, but when love contradicts our sense of fairness, we are angry. Yes, we're all in favor of God's love, but he can't love one person more than another, can he? God simply can't forgive you more than he forgives me, can he? If God's love is unfair, then it is far more offensive and far more mysterious than we ever could have imagined. The landowner's unfairness was great news to those who were unemployed with no hope of being hired. God's love may be "unfair," but when his "unfairness" includes you and me, who wants to argue?

There are many examples of God's unfair love in the Bible. The prodigal son, Zaccheus the tax collector, and the woman caught in adultery qualify, but the most outrageous example is the thief on the cross.

No more chances for the thief. No more appeals. No last-minute legal maneuvers. No possibility of rescue or a miracle. Luke tells us the thief knew he was guilty and knew he was getting what he deserved. The law was fair. This man had violated the law, and now he had to pay. But there, next to him, was Jesus. He was not being treated fairly. Everyone understood what was really going on, that his death penalty was all about power and politics. Even a thief knows innocence when he sees it. Even a thief knows the difference between fair and unfair. But the heart cannot always remain silent. Sometimes the longings which live there force their way into our voices. The thief blurts out to Jesus, "Remember me when you come into your kingdom."

Can you imagine what the thief must have been thinking? *What did I just say? What is the matter with me? I'm lost, man, I'm finished. My life is over. My luck finally ran out. I don't even know this guy next to me except ... I feel like I do. Innocence reeks from his torn body. And his eyes, they see right through me. The attraction to him is unbearable; I can't stop looking at him!*

What did I say again? Oh yeah, "Remember me!" I can't believe I said that. Why would he remember me? What would innocence have to do with someone as contaminated as me? This makes no sense whatsoever. I deserve what is happening to me, but here I am asking him to take me with him wherever it is he's going.

This is crazy! Some people say this Jesus guy is God. If he is, then I'm done for. One thing I learned at synagogue, God is just. God is fair.

Wait a minute, he's mumbling something. I ... I ... can't quite understand ...

"I tell you the truth, today you will be with me in paradise."

How unfair! Shouldn't the thief have been asked to repent, to make amends, to at least declare he was sorry? No lectures, no sermons, no teaching or demands for repentance, Jesus just ushers the man into the kingdom of God. Shouldn't we be more careful with the requirements for receiving grace? Apparently not.

God's Love Is Persistent

A young man (a friend of mine) and his wife had been trying to have a child for five years and had exhausted all their options. Childlessness began to hammer away at both of them. Difficult questions consumed them. How could two healthy lovers of God find themselves childless while so many women who never thought about God were having unwanted babies left and right?

Five years of God's silence began to take its toll, and then the miracle happened. The man's wife became pregnant! Within a few months, the news got even better: she was carrying twins.

The landscape of the couple's faith changed radically. Gone were their questions. God was good, and God was visible. Now the five years of waiting made sense! God had been teaching them to wait and now was giving them more than they had asked for. Life was good. Life made sense!

Then the unraveling began.

During a routine checkup, the doctor discovered serious problems. One of the babies had already died; the other had little chance of surviving. If it did live, it would probably suffer severe disabilities. Abortion was the only way out, the doctor said.

The bottom dropped out of my friend's life. He felt devastated, angry, frustrated, hurt, confused, and hopelessly lost in his grief. How could God do this? What kind of a God gives you a gift, and then destroys it? My friend was hanging on to his faith by a very thin piece of thread. In fact, he would say later that his faith was hanging on to him. *He* had long since let go.

Friends at his church noted his deep exhaustion and strongly encouraged him to try to pick up the pieces of his life. He accompanied me on a week of silent retreat, but he made it clear he did not want to be there and didn't try to hide his anger.

One of the spiritual exercises during the retreat was a nature walk. The spiritual director instructed us to look for places in nature where we could see God. It made my friend furious.

"This is stupid," he said. "As far as I am concerned, God is not anywhere. I am not going to waste an hour trying to find God in nature. I have been wasting the last few months trying to find God in my life, and I have received no response."

He made up his mind that he would refuse to participate in the nature walk. He would walk, all right; he would *look* like he was participating; but he would sabotage the experience by finding a long stairway of cement where he would walk, gazing only at the cement. He would not look at any plants. He would spend an hour in quiet rebellion, staring at the bleak, smooth cement.

After the exercise, he returned to his small group to describe what had happened.

"I was about halfway up the walkway," he said, "walking very slowly, lost in my anger and resentment toward God, when the tears began. I was not conscious of my tears until my mind caught up with my heart. There were cracks in the cement. The entire walkway was covered with cracks. I realized my tears were not because of the cracks; they were caused by what was *in* the cracks—in *every* crack, a flower! Somehow, in the midst of the gray lifeless cement, *life made its way* through the impenetrable rock and mortar of the sidewalk! Suddenly I was conscious of God. He was alive! He surprised me with his flowers. He found a way to show me hope in the midst of despair. His love and care had found me."

Somehow in the ruins of a man's life, while rage swirled within him, while he languished in despair, even while he was rejecting God, *God kept the conversation going.* God chased my friend into his arms.

The Annoying Conga Drum

At a recent spiritual retreat with my oldest son, the conga drum experience resurfaced. Late one evening in the middle of the retreat, I told the story to my son for the first time. The scar on my soul still remained. On the final day of the retreat, just before communion, I led a short devotional. Although I had prepared a few notes, the talk was mostly spontaneous, and the story of the conga drum spilled out of me as an illustration of something I was talking about. Neither my son nor I had expected the story to be told.

When I finished, I sat down to prepare for communion. The hushed chapel reflected our anticipation of the sacrament. The long silence continued, when, without warning, my son stomped to the front of the chapel, making an unusual amount of noise. He certainly grabbed everyone's attention. After loudly marching up the stairs to the platform, he disappeared behind a large oak podium and started rustling through papers and cardboard, searching for something. Suddenly he turned to face the audience, holding in his hands a large, shiny new conga drum. He marched forward and placed the conga drum on the altar.

Tears filled my eyes as I sat there, stunned. *Is this for me? Can I keep the conga drum?* Logic insisted that although this was a beautiful gesture from my son, it really wasn't mine to keep. *How could it be? He didn't have any idea I was going to talk about the drum. I know, he must have remembered a conga drum in the storage room backstage and spontaneously decided it would be a great way to close the service.* Clearly it was not mine to keep, so I did not reach for the drum. I wasn't about to have to give it back again.

I will never forget what happened next. From the back of the room I heard the words, "Take the conga drum!" Slowly I rose to the altar and stared through tears at the most beautiful conga drum I had ever seen. I did not pick it up; I surrounded it with my arms and hugged it off the altar. My son told me later he was going to tell the story and present me with the drum, but when I started telling the story, he realized God had orchestrated the morning far beyond anyone's expectations.

On top of the bookcase behind me sits the conga drum. Forty-seven years is a long time to wait, but the waiting is over. Each time I look at it, my heart laughs over a God who conspired to make sure I understand forever his fathomless grace. Every day, I hear him whisper, "I'll never take back my grace!"

I hope you hear him whispering too.

epilogue

I had just finished speaking at a church retreat in some faraway town back east, where I had spent three sessions pleading with the congregation to bring their busy, lopsided lives to Jesus. As soon as the last meeting was over, I had raced to the airport to catch my plane. Unfortunately, my flight was delayed, and by the time I reached San Francisco, I had missed my connection, and it would be hours before the next available flight.

I collapsed emotionally. I was stuck inside a crowded, noisy airport, and I wanted to be home with my wife. I was imprisoned by guilt for abandoning my wife, for speaking too much—you name it, I felt guilty about it. I was depressed and angry and didn't have the spiritual resources to deal with it.

Then it occurred to me that my son and daughter-in-law lived just a few miles from the airport. I could call them and talk to my grandson. *Talking with him is guaranteed to cheer me up,* I thought.

"Hello, Noah," I said.

"Ih habon ith dada," the little voice mumbled.

Life is cruel. Children just learning how to speak should not be talking to fifty-six-year-olds who are losing their hearing. At my age, little children's voices are the voices I most need to hear.

I decided to use the tried-and-tested grandparent trick: go with phonetics and fake it.

"You are playing with Dada?"

It worked.

"Dada! Pluh da twain!"

"You're playing with your train?" I was on a roll.

"Tain! Tain! Muffo grotos!"

Muffo grotos? I was desperate now. "Mommy is there too?"

"No. No. *Muffo grotos!*" The two-year-old equivalent of "Can't you understand English?"

I realized there was no hope now. Not only was I delayed from getting home, I was an inadequate grandfather who was incapable of hearing his own grandson. My gloomy disposition became gloomier. There was only one way out.

"Let me talk to Daddy, Noah!"

There was a long silence. My frustration was building.

Great! Noah is not searching for Daddy; Noah has abandoned the telephone and is playing with his train. I am stuck in this airport, and the telephone is lying on the floor! Who knows how long it will lie there!

Now I was frustrated *and* furious! I would wait one more minute, and then I would hang up. But as I started to put the phone down, Noah's tiny voice spoke as clearly as any voice I have ever heard. "I love you, Grandpa!"

My eyes filled with tears, and they would not stop. My gloom disappeared. My frustrations vanished. The darkness receded and light filled my soul. My grandson had spoken the only words my too-busy life needed to hear. With merely four words, he helped me put into perspective my delayed flight, my bad hearing, my increasing anxiety, and my lopsided schedule. "I love you, Grandpa" was all I needed to hear.

Life is complicated. Our schedules are hectic. Following Jesus is not always easy, nor is he easy to hear in the noisiness of our lives. Spirituality can be hard on our bones. My fervent prayer is that throughout this book, you heard the crystal-clear voice of Jesus whispering, "I love you." May you hear him in your unfinishedness, your incompleteness, your incompetence, in other words, in your particular mess. He's there, you know.

notes

Chapter 1: Messy

1. Genesis 9:20–28.
2. Luke 9:51–56.
3. Anne Lamott, *Traveling Mercies: Some Thoughts on Faith* (New York: Pantheon, 1999), 49–50.

Chapter 2: Messy Spirituality

1. Hebrews 12:2.
2. Barbara Brown Taylor, *The Preaching Life* (Boston: Cowley, 1993), 110–12.
3. Ron Lee Davis, *A Forgiving God in an Unforgiving World* (Eugene, Ore.: Harvest House, 1984), 63.

Chapter 3: Resisting the Resisters

1. Luke 18:35–42.

2. Shel Silverstein, *Where the Sidewalk Ends* (New York: Harper and Row, 1974), 153.

3. Don McCullough, *The Trivialization of God* (Colorado Springs: NavPress, 1995), 37.

4. Brennan Manning, *Lion and Lamb* (Old Tappan, N.J., Chosen, 1986), 172–73.

5. John 8:1–11, emphasis added.

6. Ron Lee Davis, *Mistreated* (Portland, Ore.: Multnomah Press, 1989), 85–86.

Chapter 4: The Ugliness of Rejection

1. Mike Riddell, *alt.spirit@metro.m3: Alternative Spirituality for the Third Millennium* (Oxford: Lion, 1997), 135–39.

2. Rich Wilkerson, *Straight Answers to Tough Questions about Sex* (Springdale, Pa.: Whitaker, 1987), 213–17.

Chapter 5: Odd Discipleship

1. Robert Fulghum, *Uh-Oh* (New York: Villard, 1991), 35–38.

2. C. S. Lewis, *The Lion, the Witch and the Wardrobe* (New York: Collier, 1950), 137.

3. Matthew 10:5–42.

4. If you are disturbed by the young boy's lying, check out the parable of the shrewd manager in Luke 16:1–9.

5. Dan Taylor, *Letters to My Children* (Downers Grove, Ill.: InterVarsity Press, 1989), 13–17.

Chapter 6: Unspiritual Growth

1. Doug Webster, *The Easy Yoke* (Colorado Springs: NavPress, 1995), 136–37.

2. Philippians 3:12–14 MESSAGE.

3. As told in Dr. Monroe's lecture at the Youth Specialties 1994 National Youth Worker's Convention.

4. Not an actual story but a composite of many nursing home experiences during my tenure as pastor.

Chapter 7: Little Graces

1. Wayne Rice, comp., *Hot Illustrations for Youth Talks* (Grand Rapids: Youth Specialties/Zondervan, 2001), 176–77.

2. Mark 12:41–44.

3. Told to me by Brewster McLeod, Lexington, Kentucky.

Chapter 8: God's Annoying Love

1. Romans 8:38–39, emphasis added.

2. William Barclay, *The Daily Study Bible* (Philadelphia: Westminster, 1954), 135.

3. Matthew 20:1–16.

Dynamic Communicators Workshop

Prepare with Focus, Deliver with Clarity, Speak with Power

*For youth workers, pastors,
business leaders—for anyone
who speaks to groups and
wants to do it more effectively*

Filmed live at Ken Davis's popular Dynamic Communicators Workshop, this four-tape video series (over 5 hours of quality instruction) includes the core curriculum that has helped thousands of youth workers transform their speaking. Lessons include:

- **The SCORRE method of preparation:** Learn to prepare your talk with crystal clear focus. This foundational technique has been taught, tested, and refined over the last 15 years. It has revolutionized the effectiveness of thousands of pastors, youth workers, and other speakers.

- **Illustrations:** The best illustrations aren't found in books, on the Internet, or "borrowed" from other speakers. The best illustrations are right in front of your eyes. Learn how to find and use new, powerful illustrations hiding in everyday life—illustrations that will make your talks unforgettable.

- **Body talk:** Your eyes, face, and body communicate as much or more than your words. Learn how to use an expressive face, meaningful gestures, and powerful eye contact to enhance your communication.

- **Putting it all together:** Learn how to create openings that grab and hold the attention of your listeners. Learn how to use unforgettable closings that motivate students to action. Learn powerful time-management techniques that will forever replace last-minute cramming.

The four videotapes in this series, combined with the interactive participant's guide, will help you to:

- Prepare your youth talks with focus
- Deliver your youth talks with clarity
- Speak with power

Curriculum Kit
4 videos: 5 hours, 55 minutes
ISBN: 0-310-23726-2

GRAND RAPIDS, MICHIGAN 49530

WWW.ZONDERVAN.COM

Who Is Youth Specialties?

For 30 years Youth Specialties has worked alongside Christian youth workers of just about every denomination and youth-serving organization. We're here to help you, whether you're brand new to youth ministry or a veteran, whether you're a volunteer or a career youth pastor. Each year we serve more than 100,000 youth workers and pastors worldwide through our training seminars and conventions, resources, and on the Internet.

"Youth Specialties isn't about numbers, it's about souls," says Mike Yaconelli, cofounder of the San Diego—based organization. "We do what we do to give youth workers what they need—encouragement to help them get up in the morning, and the training and resources they need to help them change the world, one kid at a time."

"Years ago I was drowning in my youth ministry. No one appreciated me, I didn't think I was making any difference with my kids, and I wanted to quit. I gotta say YS saved my life! You encouraged me and equipped me. And you told me the truth even when the truth wasn't easy to hear. Thanks!"
—a seasoned youth pastor

For more information visit
www.youthspecialties.com or
visit a certified dealer near you.

ZONDERVAN™

GRAND RAPIDS, MICHIGAN 49530

WWW.ZONDERVAN.COM

Youth Specialties